PORTRAITS OF AMERICAN WOMEN

ABIGAIL SMITH ADAMS

PORTRAITS OF AMERICAN WOMEN

By

GAMALIEL BRADFORD

BOSTON AND NEW YORK

HOUGHTON MIFFLIN COMPANY

The Riverside Press Cambridge

The Riverside Press
CAMBRIDGE · MASSACHUSETTS
PRINTED IN THE U.S.A.

TO

H. F. B.

*Il y a trois choses que j'ai beaucoup aimées
et auxquelles je n'ai jamais rien compris:
les femmes, la peinture, et la musique.*

FONTENELLE

Rien ne vit que par le détail.

SAINTE-BEUVE

PREFACE

THIS book might almost be called "Portraits of New England Women," since, with the exception of Miss Willard, all of the subjects studied in it were born in New England. As I had devoted a good many years to distinguished representatives of other parts of the country, I felt at liberty to confine my researches for a brief period to souls nearer home. In the study of women it is especially difficult to obtain satisfactory material, and material affecting the lives of New England women was most readily accessible to me. At the same time, of the seven New England characters here portrayed, at least three, Harriet Beecher Stowe, Margaret Fuller Ossoli, and Louisa May Alcott, are so thoroughly identified with the country at large that one hardly thinks of their birthplace. Abigail Adams, Mary Lyon, and Emily Dickinson are known to a great number of their countrywomen and Sarah Alden Ripley ought to be so. I hope, moreover, to follow this series with another, embracing prominent women of other sections.

I am under deep obligation to various persons for assistance in my work. Mrs. Ripley's grandchildren have kindly supplied me with numerous letters, without which it would have been impossible to make an adequate study of her. Miss Charlotte A. Hedge has lent me letters of Margaret Fuller to Dr. F. H. Hedge, and the Boston Public Library has placed its valuable Ossoli manuscripts at my disposal. Mount Holyoke College has enabled me to make use of a most interesting collection of reminiscences of Mary Lyon. Mr.

C. K. Bolton has allowed me to examine the correspondence of Frances Willard with his mother, Mrs. Sarah Knowles Bolton. And Mr. McGregor Jenkins has lent me letters and has more especially furnished me with significant personal memories of Emily Dickinson. To all these collaborators I am very grateful.

GAMALIEL BRADFORD

Wellesley Hills, Massachusetts
September 30, 1919

CONTENTS

ILLUSTRATIONS

PORTRAITS OF AMERICAN WOMEN

I

ABIGAIL ADAMS

CHRONOLOGY

Abigail Smith.
Born in Weymouth, Massachusetts, November 11, 1744.
Married John Adams, October 25, 1764.
In Europe 1784–1788.
Died at Quincy, Massachusetts, October 28, 1818.

PORTRAITS OF AMERICAN WOMEN

I

ABIGAIL ADAMS

I

THE wife of President John Adams and the mother of President John Quincy Adams is sometimes accused of being more man than woman in her temperament. This is a mistake. She was a woman and a charming one, even in an age when there was no offense in saying that women differed from men in their hearts as well as in their garments.

She had a large and varied life. Starting from a peaceful New England parsonage, where she learned the love of God and good breeding, she passed a quiet girlhood, then plunged, in her early married days, into the fierce tumult of the Revolution, managed her family and estate during her husband's long periods of absence, stood at his side in the presence of the sovereigns of Europe, reigned as the president's wife over the society of Washington, and shared the long post-presidential retirement in the Quincy home. She was always adequate to every situation and said the word and did the deed that dignity and high patriotism required of her. But it is impossible to read her many letters and not feel that through it all she was charmingly and delicately a woman.

She herself understood and appreciated the softer elements of the feminine character. In England she complains somewhat of the lack of these qualities: "The softness, peculiarly characteristic of our sex, and which is so pleasing to the gentlemen, is wholly laid aside here for the masculine attire and manners of the Amazonians."[1] She herself is feminine in the deeper things of life, in the tenderness of her affection and in the bitterness of her mourning, when those she loves are lost to her, as in her profound grief over her mother's death. She is just as feminine in those lighter trifles of fashion and dress which are supposed — by men — to form the chief part of woman's conversation and correspondence.

She was a thorough woman in her domestic interests, in that busy, often trivial, care which sustains the unconscious felicity of home. She looked after her husband's comfort as well as his greatness. In the midst of shrewd advice as to his moral bearing among those

who were making the American nation, she murmurs a
housewife's anxiety about his personal appearance: "I
feel concerned lest your clothes should go to rags, having nobody to take any care of you in your long absence;
and then, you have not with you a proper change for
the seasons."[2] She feels, sometimes a little impatiently,
the hurry of nothing which makes up domestic life.
Her health? She believes she has little health. "Much
of an invalid,"[3] she calls herself casually, and elsewhere
admits that her "health is infirm," and that she is not
"built for duration."[4] But, bless me, she has no time
to think about health, or talk about it, or write about it.
The machine must go as long as it will.

How apt and vivid is her sketch of the interruptions
that puncture the whole course of her home existence!
She rises at six o'clock and makes her own fire, "in
imitation of his Britannic Majesty." She calls her servants — repeatedly, and notes that in future she will hire
only those who will stir at one call. Breakfast gets on
the table. She would like to eat it. A man comes with
coal. A man comes with pigs. Another man comes for
something else, and another. Meanwhile, where is
breakfast? And what flavor has it? "Attended to all
these concerns. A little out of sorts that I could not
finish my breakfast. Note; never to be incommoded

with trifles."[5]   You think you are reading Madame de Sévigné.

Yet she loves her home with all a woman's true, deep affection.   Men often claim a speciality of home loving and decry a woman's restlessness.   They do not realize that they shake off the burden of life when they enter their own doors.   A woman takes it up.   Yet few men's love is really deeper than a woman's for the home she has created and every day sustains.   It was so with this lady.   There are cares, indeed.   But what is life without cares?   "I have frequently said to my friends, when they have thought me overburdened with care, I would rather have too much than too little.   Life stagnates without action."[6]   And though she saw and knew all the diversions of society and all the heights and depths of the great outer world, she clung steadfastly to the simplest maxim of a woman's heart.   "Well-ordered home is my chief delight, and the affectionate, domestic wife, with the relative duties which accompany that character, my highest ambition."[7]

And as she was a woman in her love of home, so she was thoroughly a woman in her love of her children and in her care for them.   If they are ill, she watches at their bedsides with the tenderest solicitude, delights in their recovery, and mourns almost beyond consolation when one is untimely snatched away. She herself superintends their early studies, and most thoughtfully and carefully. She does indeed regret her own lack of book learning, because she has none to impart to her daughters; but perhaps, even in this regard, she was less deficient than might be thought. She keeps little Johnny at her knee reading aloud Rollin's "Ancient History," and hopes that he will come to "entertain a fondness for it." [8] She vastly prefers Dr. Watts's "Moral Songs for Children" to modern frivolities of "Jack and Jill" and "Little Jack Horner." [9] Would she have liked "Rollo," I wonder, or would she not?

Whatever the value of her literary teaching, her moral lessons were as homely, as sturdy, and as lofty as those of a matron of Plutarch. On this point she was fully supported by the resonant precepts of her husband: "Root out every little thing. Weed out every meanness. Make them great and manly. Teach them to scorn injustice, ingratitude, cowardice, and falsehood." [10] But she needed no precepts from any one. Out of her own heart she taught these things, and her apostrophe to her son, when he left her for the great world, is simply the flower of lessons and influences established many years before: "Dear as you are to me, I would much rather you should have found your grave in the ocean you have crossed, or that any untimely death should crop you in your infant years, than see you an immoral, profligate, or graceless child." [11]

If one wants evidence of this maternal loftiness and maternal tenderness combined, one has only to open the Diary of John Quincy Adams and to see how reverent, how affectionate, and how obviously sincere are the numerous references to his mother's care and devotion. "My mother was an angel upon earth. She was a minister of blessing to all human beings within her sphere of action. . . . She has been to me more than a mother. She has been a spirit from above watching over me for good, and contributing by my mere consciousness of her existence to the comfort of my life." [12] "There is not a virtue that can abide in the female heart but it was the ornament of hers." [13] Yet the younger Adams was not one inclined to overestimate human nature, even in those most nearly bound to him. His devotion to his mother's memory was as persistent as it was profound. When he himself had reached his seventy-sixth year, the mere reading of some of her letters threw him into a state of singular excitement. "I actually sobbed as he read, utterly unable to suppress my emotion. Oh, my mother! Is there anything on earth so affecting to me as thy name? so precious as thy instructions to my childhood, so dear as the memory of thy life?" [14]

We may safely say, then, that this was a true woman in her home and with her children. She was a woman likewise in the freshness and vivacity of her social relations. When she writes to her granddaughter, "Cultivate, my dear, those lively spirits and that sweet innocence and contentedness, which will rob the desert of its gloom, and cause the wilderness to bloom around you," [15] we know that she herself had cultivated these things with assiduity and success. She was in no way dependent upon society and there were times when she distinctly shrank from it, when its duties were a burden and its forms and ceremonials a wearisome embarrassment. Her happiest, sunniest hours were no doubt passed with her husband and children in the busy retirement of her Quincy home. But at different periods of her life she was called upon to mingle in all sorts of social circles, the loftiest as well as the most brilliant, and everywhere she bore herself with the grace and ease and dignity of a refined and accomplished lady.

She had those most essential ingredients of the social spirit, a woman's quick sense of the varied interest of human character and a woman's sympathetic insight into the workings of the human heart. And she had, also, a rare power of expression, so that her account of striking scenes and distinguished people has often something of the snap and sparkle of Lady Mary Montagu or Madame de Sévigné. How admirable, for instance, is her picture of Madame Helvétius, the friend of Franklin, ending, "I hope, however, to find amongst the French ladies manners more consistent with my ideas of decency, or I shall be a mere recluse."[16] Or, for a briefer sketch, take that of Mrs. Cranch, who is "a little, smart, sprightly, active woman and is wilted just enough to last to perpetuity."[17]

And Mrs. Adams's thorough womanliness showed not only in her personal relations, in her daily interests, in her social glitter and vivacity, but in deeper and more subtle sensibilities, which many true women are without. She had an excellent control over her nerves, was quite capable of stoical heroism, as we shall see later, but the nerves were there and show, through all her mastery. She would have readily admitted, with the lady of Shakespeare,

I am a woman, therefore full of fears.

Or, as she herself puts it, "I never trust myself long with the terrors which sometimes intrude themselves upon me."[18] The nerves responded to all sorts of other suggestions also. To art perhaps not so much. The early training of Puritan New England did not altogether fit nerves for æsthetic sensibility. Yet her enthusiasm over the opera in Paris is far more than a mere conventional ecstasy, and the possibilities of music for her are richly indicated in a casual sentence: "I cannot describe to you how much I was affected the other day with a Scotch song, which was sung to me by a young lady in order to divert a melancholy hour." [19]

Nature touched her even more than music. The poets she knew were those of the eighteenth century and her formal description has rather too much of eighteenth-century zephyrs and vernal airs. But it is easy to get through this to her real, deep love of bare New England pastures and wide meadows and the homely country-side that had woven itself into her life. And as the nerves thrilled to old Scotch airs, so they quivered and melted under the coming of May days. "The approach of spring unstrings my nerves, and the south winds have the same effect upon me which Brydone says the Sirocco winds have upon the inhabitants of Sicily." [20]

In short, she was a shifting, varying, mercurial creature, as perhaps we all are, but she certainly more than many of us. "Oh, why," she exclaims, "was I born with so much sensibility, and why, possessing it, have I so often been called to struggle with it?" [21] One moment she is "lost and absorbed in a flood of tenderness." [22] The next "my heart is as light as a feather and

my spirits are dancing." [23]   To-day she writes: "I am
a mortal enemy to anything but a cheerful countenance and a merry heart." [24]   And then to-morrow: "I
have many melancholy hours, when the best company
is tiresome to me and solitude the greatest happiness
I can enjoy." [25]

So it can hardly be claimed that she was too stoical
and too philosophical and too stern-hearted to be a
woman.

II

BUT Mrs. Adams lived in a tremendous time.   In her
early married years her husband's political duties left
her alone to do both her work and his in the midst of
difficulty and danger.   Later she was called upon to
stand by his side through great crises of statesmanship
and to give him counsel in triumph and comfort in defeat.   She performed all these functions nobly, and to do
it required something more than the usual feminine con-
tributions to domestic felicity.   She had a woman's
heart, a woman's nerves, a woman's tenderness; but
little indeed of what a man requires to make his way in
life was lacking to her.

She had a high and fine intelligence.   Elaborate education she had not, nor any woman in that day.   She

herself complains that she was not sent to school, that
ill health prevented any systematic mental training, that
reading and writing and the simplest arithmetic, with
a few accomplishments, were all that was thought necessary for her or any of her sex. In later life she be-
wailed this state of things and urged that a wide and
rational spiritual culture was as necessary and as suit-
able for women as for men.

But we all know that education does not make intelligence and that natural intelligence can supply almost
everything that education gives to either man or woman.
After all, schooling is but an inadequate and apologetic
substitute for brains. Brains Mrs. Adams had, and
needed no substitute. From her childhood her keen
and active wit was working, observing, acquiring, re-
jecting, laying by for future use. She was always a
wide reader,—read and quoted Shakespeare and Pope
and the eighteenth-century poets and essayists. Her
acuteness and independence of judgment are well shown
in this comment on the Drama of Molière: "I send
with this the first volume of Molière and should be glad
of your opinion of them. I cannot be brought to like
them. It seems to me to be a general want of spirit,
at the close of every one I have felt disappointed. There
are no characters but what appear unfinished and he

seems to have ridiculed vice without engaging us to virtue; and though he sometimes makes us laugh, yet 't is a smile of indignation. . . .   Molière is said to have been an honest man, but sure he has not copied from his own heart.   Though he has drawn many pictures of real life, yet all pictures of life are not to be exhibited upon the stage." [26]   Above all, she read the classics, of course in translation; even writers minor or less known, like Polybius.   Plutarch she nourished her heart on, and when she signed her letters to her husband, " Portia," it was partly an eighteenth-century affectation, but much more that the iron of old Roman virtue had entered into the very substance of her soul.

Also, her intelligence reached far beyond books.   She had that penetrating, analytical instinct which plucks wisdom from the actions and motives of men and which especially lays the foundation of such wisdom in a close, dispassionate study of the observer's own heart.   " You know I make some pretensions to physiognomy," [27] she writes.   The pretensions were justified.   She saw many faces in her life and read them attentively, curiously, and always with profit.

But the finest testimony to Mrs. Adams's intelligence is the letters addressed to her by her husband and her son.   Both were men of wide and deep reflection.   Both

touched perpetually the gravest problems of statesmanship and of human conduct generally. Both discussed
these problems with wife and mother as they would
have discussed them together, or with the wisest men
of their time. Would this have been possible with
any but a mind of the broadest grasp and keenest
power of comprehension?

And the intelligence was progressive as well as vigorous. Mrs. Adams's energetic protest to her husband
against the legal and political subjection of women in
that day has been often quoted and justly praised, — it
is as dignified as it is energetic: "That your sex are
naturally tyrannical is a truth so thoroughly established
as to admit of no dispute," [28] and she urges such an
adjustment of law as may check that tyranny. In religious matters there is the same broad, sober common-
sense. Mrs. Adams had been brought up in the strictest
New England Calvinism, and always retained the intense earnestness of that creed and its disposition to
try all things by the standard of conscience. But bigotry and intellectual cowardice were alike abhorrent to
her, and she had no inclination to judge others harshly.
"True, genuine religion is calm in its inquiries, deliberate in its resolves, and steady in its conduct." [29] And
besides common-sense she infused into her piety some-

thing of that sunshine which was the sorest need of Calvinism and for want of which it perished: "I am one of those who are willing to rejoice always. My disposition and habits are not of the gloomy kind. I believe that 'to enjoy is to obey.'" [30]

But vigorous and clear as Mrs. Adams's mind was in the abstract, its energy showed still more in practical matters, as was natural and necessary with the life she lived. We have seen that she could be perfectly contented with simple home surroundings and regular pursuits. But she wanted neither sloth nor lethargy. "Confinement does not suit me or my family," [31] she wrote to her granddaughter. And again: "Man was made for action, and for bustle, too, I believe. I am quite out of conceit with calms." [32] She had her share of furious housewifery, and no sooner gets on shipboard than she sets to work with "scrapers, mops, brushes, infusions of vinegar, etc.," [33] to produce the neatness and order which she maintained daily at home without such appeal to violent measures.

And her domestic economy went far beyond mops and brushes. During her husband's long and necessary absences, she undertook not only the ordinary duties of wife and mother, but the general management of farms and property, and performed these functions most efficiently, as is shown by the commendation which she receives from her loving partner quite as frequently as advice. She makes purchases and sales, she hires help, she garners crops. Through it all she carries her own burden and avoids, so far as possible, filling her letters with complaints. "I know the weight of public cares lie so heavy upon you that I have been loath to mention your own private ones." [34]

In dealing with that greatest and ever-present and insoluble problem of married and all other life, money, Mrs. Adams herself asserts that she was thrifty and prudent. So do all the rest of us, all man and womankind. But in this case I think we may believe the statement. There was certainly no niggardliness. The husband was too large for petty cheese-paring. "You know I never get or save anything by cozening or classmating," [35] he writes, and his wife was like him. She maintained a sober decency and propriety in her own expenditure, and through all the cramped revolutionary time, when dollars were even rarer than hope, she always kept and used the means of relieving those whose straits were worse than her own. But she understood thoroughly both the theory of economy and its practice. Few professional students would have analyzed financial conditions more keenly than she does in the long letter written to her husband at an early stage of the war.[36]   And the practical strain shows in her simple statement: "I have studied, and do study, every method of economy in my power; otherwise a mint of money would not support a family."[37]

Certainly, without any intention of boasting, she herself, in her later years, sums up her usefulness to husband and children when she is explaining to her sister the multiplicity of care that seems to hang around her as thickly in age as it did in youth: "You know, my dear sister, if there be bread enough, and to spare, unless a prudent attention manage that sufficiency, the fruits of diligence will be scattered by the hand of dissipation.   No man ever prospered in the world without the consent and coöperation of his wife."[38]

As she had patience to endure want and privation, so she had courage to meet danger.   When those she loves are in peril, her heart feels "like a heart of lead."[39]   But for herself, sensitive as her nerves may be, there is a strain of heroism which swells and hardens at the touch of emergency.   The anticipation of evils makes her doubt a little.   "If danger comes near my dwelling, I suppose I shall shudder."[40]   But when her husband writes to her, "In case of real danger, of which you cannot fail to have previous intimations, fly to the woods with our children,"[41] we know, we see, that she would have had perfect presence of mind either to fly or to remain, as the wisest courage might dictate. "I am not suddenly elated or depressed,"[42] she says; and again, "I am not apt to be intimidated."[43] Though she was far from given to self-commendation, she declares solemnly that if the men are not able to perform their duty to their country, the enemy will find the women to be a veritable race of Amazons. Nay, she even goes forth as a spectator and enjoys one of the most fierce, intense excitements known to man, the vision of a field of battle. "I have just returned from Penn's hill, where I have been sitting to hear the amazing roar of cannon, and from whence I could see every shell which was thrown. The sound, I think, is one of the grandest in nature, and is of the true species of the sublime."[44]

Do not, however, set this lady down as one who would have taken a bloodthirsty delight in bull-fights or the prize ring. If she hearkened with a thrill of awed pleasure to the booming of cannon, it was because they were fired in defense of her country and of liberty. She knew well what her friends and fellow citizens were fighting for, and if she took a passionate interest in the struggle, it was because her whole heart and hopes were fixed upon the end of it. Her husband's letters

to her contain much lucid statement and analysis of
the methods and aims of the Revolution, and hers are
scarcely behind his in clear understanding and intensity
of purpose.

She thought much, and thought with broad intelligence on general political questions, liked to talk of
them, liked to write of them. "Well, you tell H. she
must not write politics; now it is just as natural for
me to fall upon them as to breathe."[45] She has no
illusions about democracy, or about human nature,—
speaks at times even with cynical insight of its failures
and defects. The lamentable inconsistencies of statesmanship are not hidden from her. How many who
were fighting for American freedom at that day had
the courage to cry out that it was absurd for men who
kept slaves to take up arms and fight battles in the name
of liberty? Mrs. Adams had that courage.[46]

Yet, in spite of the selfishness of politicians and the
inadequacy of human ideals, this wise and energetic
woman never faltered for a moment in her devotion
to the cause of her country, never wavered in her hope.
The warmth and the glory of her enthusiasm must have
been a splendid comfort to her husband and to all who
knew her. Her passion does, indeed, occasionally de-
generate into bitterness against her enemies. Alas, we

do not need recent examples to show us that this is too easy with even the wisest and the noblest. "Those who do not scruple to bring poverty, misery, slavery, and death upon thousands will not hesitate at the most diabolical crimes," she writes; "and this is Britain."[47] But she has the same noble scorn for folly and meanness on her own side. "If our army is in ever so critical a state, I wish to know it. . . . If all America is to be ruined and undone by a pack of cowards and knaves, I wish to know it. Pitiable is the lot of their commander."[48] And her words of counsel, of confidence, of inspiration, are never wanting. Her young brother-in-law longs to enter the army. She pleads and reasons with his doubting mother to make her permit it. Her husband is involved in an endless tangle of difficulty and danger. She would not have him shun an hour of it. "You cannot be, I know, nor do I wish to see you, an inactive spectator; but if the sword be drawn, I bid adieu to all domestic felicity, and look forward to that country where there are neither wars nor rumors of war, in a firm belief, that through the mercy of its King we shall both rejoice there together."[49] Nor does she urge others to sacrifices which she is unwilling to make herself. Foreign luxuries? Let them go. Plain milk makes as good a breakfast as sugared coffee. Not

one of the comforts to which she has been accustomed
but she will cheerfully renounce. If the men are taken
from the fields, the women will do the work for them.
She herself doubts her strength for digging potatoes,
but she can gather corn and husk it. What she can
do, she will do, that her children and her children's
children may be free.

III

MRS. ADAMS'S interesting combination of a true
woman's gentleness and sensibility with the masculine
qualities called for by her time is best studied, as some
of the preceding quotations indicate, in her relation to
her husband. To understand this relation fully, it is
necessary to have some idea of his very marked and
peculiar character. He was, then, a man of broad intellectual power, of keen insight into political and moral
problems, of energetic and self-sacrificing patriotism.
He commanded the respect of all men by his dignity,
his courage, his sincerity of speech and action, his entire honesty. But men did not love him; for he had
not tact; he had not social charm; he bristled with egotism, and, like many egotists, he was morbidly sensitive
and showed it. I do not know any one quotation that
much better depicts the man than the following: "I

have a very tender, feeling heart. This country knows
not, and never can know, the torments I have endured
for its sake. I am glad it never can know, for it would
give more pain to the benevolent and humane than I
could wish even the wicked and malicious to feel." [50]
Try to imagine Washington saying that.

Also, John Adams was a man who found fault with
everything, and therefore naturally he found fault with
his wife. Even his praise too often savors of patronage
and his advice is apt to carry a strong taint of criticism. Occasionally he flings out in undisguised dis-
pleasure. Though she was the last person to complain
of her health, he cannot resist a sarcasm about it: "My
wife has been sick all winter, frequently at the point
of death, in her own opinion." [51] Her indiscretion in
money matters, though at a time when discretion was
almost impossible, provokes him to sharp reproof.
"How could you be so imprudent? You must be frugal,
I assure you." [52] But the best is the incident of the
young coach horses, driven imprudently to church and
causing a most indecorous disturbance there. Mrs.
Adams was not present herself, but she authorized the
proceeding, and the husband notes, in hot wrath, "I
scolded at the coachman first, and afterwards at his
mistress, and I will scold again and again; it is my

duty."[53] Perhaps a husband to whom scolding is a duty is even worse than one to whom it is a pleasure.

Nevertheless, this husband, who could scold and be imperious and even tyrannical, like others, adored and reverenced and obeyed his wife, like others. How pretty are his compliments to her wit and intelligence, though he veils them under sarcasm. Of a certain acquaintance he says: "In large and mixed companies she is totally silent, as a lady ought to be. But whether her eyes are so penetrating, and her attention so quick to the words, looks, gestures, sentiments, etc., of the company, as yours would be, saucy as you are this way, I won't say."[54] And there is no trace of sarcasm in the ample admission to his son that in all the vicissitudes of fortune his wife had been his help and comfort, while without her he could not have endured and survived. In a letter written to his granddaughter the same enthusiasm appears, even more nobly. He compares his wife to the heroic Lady Russell, who stood by her husband's side in times equally troublous. "This lady," he says, "was more beautiful than Lady Russell, had a brighter genius, more information, a more refined taste, and [was] at least her equal in the virtues of the heart."[55]

An extensive correspondence, covering many years,

reveals to us fully Mrs. Adams's relations with this
companion of her long life, reveals her love and anxiety
and devotion and enthusiasm for the man to whom
she early gave her whole heart and from whom she
never withdrew it for a moment. As he rises in the
world, becomes a guide and a leader, a prominent citi-
zen, a great historical figure, she accompanies him in
spirit always, with watchful care, with fruitful caution,
with delicate suggestion. She sighs over the necessities of state which part her from him. She slights, as
we all do, great gifts of fortune that we have, and
deplores those that are denied her. She hoped to have
married a man, not a title, she says. A humble, private station with a husband would have been sweeter
than grandeur without one. Yet we know well enough
that she would not have had him lose an inch of fortune for her comfort, and never woman developed more
fully the grace and ease and dignity which great station
requires than did she. The letter she wrote him on
the day of his inauguration as president has been often
cited and deserves citation. It is a noble letter. "My
feelings are not those of pride or ostentation, upon the
occasion. They are solemnized by a sense of the obligations, the important trusts, and numerous duties connected with it. That you may be enabled to discharge

them with honor to yourself, with justice and impartiality to your country, and with satisfaction to this great people, shall be the daily prayer of your A. A."[56]

And as she was perfectly adapted to share her husband's greatness, so she accepted with equal composure and dignity his comparative failure and downfall. She did not seek honors and glories, she says, and she is quite content to part from them. A peaceful life at Quincy, with the man she loves, is all she ever asked for, and nothing can be more delightful than to have it given back to her. We know how much of sincerity there is in such declarations and how much of creditable and fine mendacity. In Mrs. Adams they were probably as sincere as they ever are. She was a sincere woman. But though she was perfectly ready to accept her husband's defeat, she could not quite forgive those who, in her opinion, had conspired against him and betrayed him. Toward such political enemies her language is not wholly free from a certain ungracious, if pardonable, acerbity. Thus, she says of one who should have been beneath her contempt, "I hear that Duane has got hold of my letter to Niles, and spits forth vulgar abuse at me . . . but the low sarcasms of these people affect me no more at this day than the idle wind."[57]

Even in regard to Jefferson her animosity was long a-dying. In early days she had known him well and admired and loved him. Then the fierce political contest which made him her husband's successor parted them. Between the two men the feud was soon forgotten, and the long correspondence of their old age, crowned by their deaths on the same anniversary of American independence, is one of the striking traditions of our history. But Mrs. Adams forgave more slowly than her husband. When Jefferson, who had always admired her and who spoke of her as "one of the most estimable characters on earth,"[58] finally made a direct appeal to their former affection, she answered him with courtesy, but with a clear, vigorous, burning logic that showed how deep and unhealed the old wound was: Jefferson's conduct, she says, she "considered as a personal injury." Then she ends, as a Christian should: "I bear no malice. I cherish no enmity. I would not retaliate if it was in my power."[59] But nobody is left in a moment's doubt as to what she felt.

Through all these accidents and floods of fortune it is easy to observe how great at once and how unobtrusive was Mrs. Adams's influence over her husband. She never dreamed of any vulgar domination, or desired it. She knew well the limits of her activity and

his and respected them.   Her advice, when given at
all, was given discreetly, tentatively, and, without being
in any way enforced, was left with time to prove its
value.   Time did prove its value, and in consequence
the recipient of it came to look for more and to depend
upon it more than he knew, perhaps more than even
she herself knew.

Yet in all that concerned their personal relations, as
indeed in all that concerned human nature, her knowledge was far finer and more delicate than his.   It was
just this exquisite comprehension of his character and
temperament that made her counsel of such constant
utility.   To be sure, her means of information were
greater, as well as her faculty of insight.   He had little
reserve, with her at any rate, spoke out his needs and
hopes and discouragements, made plain his strength and
weakness, unrolled his heart like a scroll before her
searching and tender scrutiny.   This she could not do.
She felt more than he those mighty, subtle barriers
which seal the tongue and make it incapable of utter-
ing what it yearns to utter.   In one of her letters occurs
this simple statement which says so much: "My pen is
always freer than my tongue.   I have written many
things to you that I suppose I never could have
talked." [60]   Yet even her pen is tongue-tied in compari-

son with his. Therefore it is evident that much of her is beyond his divination, while she sees clear into every corner of his heart, understands what affection there is, what power there is, what weakness there is, understands just exactly the weight and significance there is in those scoldings delivered again and again from a sense of duty. Must we add that she saw all this partly from finer vision and partly from greater eagerness, while he saw not only all he was fitted, but also all that he desired, to see?

For she was a woman, and her love was her whole soul; and it is a delight, after all these strayings in masculine by-paths, to return to the woman in her. She writes long letters on great matters, domestic difficulties, foreign levies, questions of policy, questions of state; but always in some brief sentence there is the heart of the letter and the heart of the woman. It is annoying sometimes to stiff, starched John. "I shall have vexations enough, as usual," he writes. "You will have anxiety and tenderness enough, as usual. Pray strive not to have too much." [61] When there is prospect of their letters being captured by the British and printed, his comment is, that they would both be made to appear very ridiculous.[62]

Ridiculous! What does she care for being ridiculous?

This is the man she worships and she wants him.   At
the very suggestion of his being ill, ten thousand horrors seize upon her imagination, and she says so.   All
he writes of state matters is very well.   She is glad
to hear it, hungers for it.   But she hungers far more
for those little tokens of tenderness which he has no
time for giving.   "Could you, after a thousand fears
and anxieties, long expectation and painful suspense, be
satisfied with my telling you that I was well, that I
wished you were with me, that my daughter sent her
duty, that I had ordered some articles for you, which
I hoped would arrive, etc., etc.?   By Heaven, if you
could, you have changed hearts with some frozen Lap-
lander, or made a voyage to a region that has chilled
every drop of your blood." [63]   Love her, oh, yes, she
knows he loves her, after his fashion, but why does n't
he say so, after her fashion?   "Every expression of
tenderness is a cordial to my heart." [64]   "I want some
sentimental effusions of the heart." [65]   The language
is the language of Addison, but the want is the want
of Eve forever.   It murmurs through these letters of
war and business like a touch of birdsong on a field of
battle.

Then, when we have got it thoroughly into our heads
that this was a woman and a lover, we can end with

her own splendid answer — appropriate at this day as
it was at that — when she was asked how she bore
having Mr. Adams absent for three years in his country's service. "If I had known, sir, that Mr. Adams
could have effected what he has done, I would not only
have submitted to the absence I have endured, painful
as it has been, but I would not have opposed it, even
though three years more should be added to the number (which Heaven avert!). I feel a pleasure in being
able to sacrifice my selfish passions to the general good,
and in imitating the example which has taught me to
consider myself and family but as the small dust of the
balance, when compared with the great community." [66]

II
SARAH ALDEN RIPLEY

CHRONOLOGY

Sarah Alden Bradford
Born in Boston, July 31, 1793.
Married Rev. Samuel Ripley, 1818.
Lived in Waltham, Massachusetts, 1818–1846.
Lived in Concord, Massachusetts, from 1846
  until her death.
Husband died, November 24, 1847.
Died in Concord, July 26, 1867.

SARAH ALDEN RIPLEY

II

SARAH ALDEN RIPLEY

I

FEW American women of to-day know of Mrs. Samuel Ripley, but a sentence from Senator Hoar's "Autobiography" will give her a favorable introduction: "She was one of the most wonderful scholars of her time, or indeed of any time. President Everett said she could fill any professor's chair at Harvard." To this we may add the testimony of Professor Child, whose authority no one will question: "The most learned woman I have ever known, the most diversely learned perhaps of her time, and not inferior in this respect, I venture to say, to any woman of any age."

It seems worth while to hear a little more about her, does it not?

From her childhood she had a passion for books and study. Every available minute was snatched for them, and some that were not available. "I never go to Boston or anywhere else, my passion for reading increasing inversely with time," she writes when little more than a child. In the early years of the nineteenth century, when she was growing up, New England was not very favorable to the education of girls — nor was any other place. But she was fortunate in having a father — Captain Bradford, of Duxbury — who was a scholar as well as a sea captain, and who loved her and liked to indulge her fancies.

"Father, may I study Latin?" she asked him.

"Latin! A girl study Latin! Certainly. Study anything you like."

Whereupon she compares him, greatly to his advantage, with another father who endeavored to convince his daughter that "all knowledge, except that of domestic affairs, appears unbecoming in a female."

Becoming or not, all knowledge was acceptable to her. She studied Latin until she could read it like a modern tongue, Greek the same, also French, German, and Italian. She did this largely alone, German without any assistance whatever, persisting incredibly, "working still at an abominable language without being sensible of the least progress," she complains. Nor did she confine herself to languages. Her zeal for mathematics and philosophy was fully equal. Most of all, perhaps, she loved the sciences; and chemistry, astronomy, and especially botany, were a delight to her from youth to age.

Nor did she take her study of languages as a task simply, as an end in itself, as so many do. It was but a means, a greater facility for getting at the thoughts of wise men and past ages. She read Latin and Greek widely as well as thoroughly. Tacitus and Juvenal must have furnished odd reflection for a schoolgirl, and it is not every infant of fourteen who regales her imagination with the novels of Voltaire.

Naturally such solitary reading in a child of that age had something academic about it, and the intellectual enthusiasm of her early letters abounds in pleasing suggestions of copy-book moralities. Yet the keen, vigorous insight often breaks through, even here. Conventional habit might lead an ordinary student to moralize on death; but few ordinary students would generalize their botanical observations into the remark that soon "our bodies, transformed into their airy elements, may be converted into the jointed stalk of the rank grass which will wave over our graves." Pretty well for a girl of sixteen!

And though she studied rules and learned traditions, and so early laid over her spirit a mighty mass of authority, she did not propose to be in any way a slave to it. When rules vex her, she cries out against them. For instance, she could never spell, and why should she? "I

wish the free spirit were not trammeled by these con-
founded rules." Also, while she studies for study's
sake, and could hardly be expected, in the early days, to
interest herself too much in the why of it, you get singular hints of penetration where you least look for
them. She asks herself whether her devotion to the
Classics springs " from pride of learning in your humble
servant or intrinsic merit in Cicero, Virgil, and Tacitus."
The question is one that many an older scholar might
put with advantage.

It is, above all, in the line of religious speculation that
one examines most curiously Sarah's gradual change
from a conventional acceptance of what is taught her
to fierce, independent thinking for herself. She was
brought up on by no means narrow lines of orthodoxy.
But in her early letters there is a serious and earnest
acceptance of the fundamental doctrines of Christianity
and a loyal effort to apply them. Gradually this unques-
tioning submission yields to the steady encroachment of
the spirit of inquiry, the "dread of enthusiasm, of the
mind's becoming enslaved to a system perhaps errone-
ous, and shut forever against the light of truth." With
the process of years the emancipation grows more
marked, until little of the old faith is left but the
unfailing habit of its goodness.

Do not, however, for a moment suppose that this studious and thoughtful childhood was altogether lost in bookishness, that Sarah was, in youth or in age, a stuffy pedant. She was never that in the least, at any time of her life; never gave that impression to any one. She was at all points an energetic, practical, efficient, common-sense human being. She did not indeed have the eager life of sport and diversion that the girl of to-day has. No girl had it then. There was no tennis or basket-ball, not even skating, or swimming, or riding. These things would not have been ladylike if they had been possible. Instead of them, there were only long walks in the Duxbury woods, the rich, wholesome flavor of the New England autumn: "The great pear tree at the gate, full of orange pears; the ground strewed with golden high-tops; the girl in the corn-barn paring apples to dry; the woods filled with huckleberries."

Also, there were the pressing cares of daily life, where mouths were many and means were little. Sarah had her full share of these and met them with swift and adequate efficiency. It is true, she groans sometimes over "that dreadful ironing day," and rebels a little when "Betsey, teasing to know how the meat is to be dissected," interferes with letters filled with Greek poets and Roman historians. But she comes right down to earth and stays there, heats the irons, dissects the meat, sweeps the parlor, at proper times takes an apparently absorbed interest in shopping and ribbons and furbelows, as a normal girl should.

Even her abstruser preoccupations are put to practical use. The oldest of a large family, she imparts her own acquirements to those who come after her, not making any one the scholar she herself was, but giving them all an education exceptional in that day or any day. Also, she gave them more than book-education; for the early death of her mother left her at the head of the household, and she attended to every duty as if her beloved books did not exist at all. Nor was she moved by the sense of duty only, but by tenderness and affection, as appears charmingly in the words written by her father to her mother from oversea: "Tell Sarah (oh, she is a seraph!) that I thank her with my tears which flow fast as I now write and think of her good behavior, her virtues, her filial piety."

To which let me add these few words from the same source, which show that she was a live, flesh-and-blood girl and not a mere copy-book model: "You I hope are skipping, jumping, dancing, and running up and down in Boston. This I know you are doing if you are well, for you are always on the wing."

Souls that skip and dance and are always on the wing usually have the elements of sociability in them. In her youth, as later, Sarah was popular and beloved by those who knew her. She had a singular charm of simplicity and grace, and if she was aroused and interested, she had that social attraction which comes when quick words spring from vivid and eager thoughts. At the same time, she never sought the world and often shunned it. Her first preoccupation was with books, and she turned to them when possible. Trivial social occasions were to be avoided on principle: "I do not intend to give up all society; I intend only to relinquish that from which I can gain no good." Moreover, she was naturally shy and self-conscious, doubted her own powers of conversation and entertainment, her own instinct of behavior in company. A dread of impropriety, she says, is the plague of her life. And again, "I should have exerted myself more, but I believe I shall never learn to talk."

She was a close analyst of her sensations and experiences with others as well as alone, and this is not a temper favorable to complete social enjoyment. The hearts of those about her she read with equal keenness — a habit also not always socially fortunate. She would not for the world have hurt the feelings of a single human being; and when she reproaches herself with talking scandal, we know that it is such scandal as one might expect from a saint. But even at an early age she saw men and women as they are, and this, alas, in our mingled life, is too often to appear ill-natured. Therefore she turned from men and women to books and thoughts. Which does not mean that she had not kindly affections, deep and tender and lasting. Here also the sharp probe of her analysis intrudes itself. To her dearest friend she says, "I love you as much as I am capable of loving any one"; and late in life she observes, "I have learned by experience that friendship is a plant that must be watered and nursed or it withers."

But these self-doubting loves often are the tenderest and truest, and Sarah's devotion to those for whom she really cared was as sincere as it was lasting. With a humility as touching as her independence, she writes to one of them, "You are the only person who ever thought me of any consequence and I am pretty well convinced that other folks are more than half right. I want you to love me, but do as you please about it."

These words were written to that singular personage, Mary Moody Emerson, aunt of Ralph Waldo and half-sister of Samuel Ripley, whom Sarah afterwards married. The friendship between these ladies was

close and warm, and Mrs. Ripley always spoke of Miss
Emerson with the greatest esteem. But one even
nearer to her was Miss Allyn, later Mrs. Francis, and
the long series of letters that passed between them is
delightful in its simplicity, its cordiality, its curious
revelation of two pure and sympathetic spirits. What
an odd mixture it presents of common daily interests,
religious aspiration, and intellectual enthusiasm! New
bonnets, old prayers, botany, chemistry, Homer and
Tacitus jostle each other on the same page with quite
transparent genuineness and charm.

The one topic supposed to be most common in young
ladies' letters, that is, young men and their doings and
their attentions, is quite absent here. The truth is,
Sarah was not concerned with such things. There is
no evidence that in her childhood and youth her heart
was ever touched. When she was twenty-five years
old, she married Mr. Ripley. She did not pretend that
it was a marriage of love on her side. She had the
greatest respect for her husband, who was a clergyman
of high and noble character in every way. Her father
was anxious for the match, and she yielded to persuasion. But at the time a life of solitary study seemed to
her preferable, as she frankly admits. The words with
which she announced her engagement, in writing to

Miss Emerson, are curiously characteristic: "Your family have probably no idea what trouble they may be entailing on themselves; I make no promises of good behavior, but knowing my tastes and habits they must take the consequences upon themselves." After which, it need merely be added that there never was a more devoted and affectionate wife.

II

I AM going to pass at once from Mrs. Ripley in youth to Mrs. Ripley in age, because in fairness I should end with the ripe perfection of her middle years. It so happens that we have abundant correspondence of the earlier and later periods, but little between, when she was too occupied and too active to write. In age as in youth her spirit was pure, lofty, and serene; but with her temperament it was natural that the sadness of age should be peculiarly apparent. The contrast cannot be better illustrated than by two very beautiful passages, written fifty years apart.

In the buoyancy of early days she writes: "A light breakfast and a ride into town in the cool morning air, stretched my existence through eternity. I lived ages in an hour." The tottering limbs and broken

thoughts of after years recall a dim echo of these rap-
tures, how far, how very far away: "I took a walk in
the pine grove near the cemetery, yesterday morning,
and crept down the hill into a deep ravine we used to
call the bowl, covered with decayed leaves, where we
used to play tea with acorns for fairy cups; the acorns
and the cups remain, but the charm is gone never to
return."

It is in this older period of her life that the impression
of Mrs. Ripley's personal appearance survives with most
of those who have told us anything about her career. It
is not said that even in youth she was especially beautiful; but in youth as in age there must have been the
suggestion of earnest purity and dignity, so marked in
all the likenesses of her that remain. Her features are
calm, thoughtful, noble, sympathetic, but with a hint
of the sadness of one who has meditated long on life
with vast comprehension and limited hope.

This impression of sadness is undeniably prominent
in the numerous letters of her later years. "Sorrow,
not hope," she says, "is the color of old age." Her
sorrow never has the shade of petulance or pitiful
complaint. It is even penetrated with a sweet kindliness that often amounts to sunshine. But the sorrow is
there, deeply motived and all-pervading.

To her clear vision it seems that all things are falling away from her. Society? The contact with her fellows had never been the chief thing in her life. Now the few she loved are gone or going, and the many who used to excite a vague curiosity have such different ways and thoughts that she can hardly understand them any more. Her last years were passed in the Manse, at Concord, the dwelling of her husband's forefathers. The Manse was then, as it has always been, widely hospitable, and the hurry of eager feet often passed her threshold and the door of her quiet chamber. She listened to it with sympathetic tenderness, but her interest faded with the fading years.

Religion? Religion had melted for her into a great love. But of active beliefs she cherished few or none. The days of strenuous thought and fierce probing of impenetrable secrets were over. She would gladly put aside the little child's questions if she could have the little child's peace. "How well it is that the world is so large, that lichens grow on every tree, that there are toadstools as well as sermons for those that like them."

Newspapers? She had rarely read them in her most active days. She could find little interest in them now. Even the turbulence of the Civil War touched her but slightly. She had drunk deep of the horrors of the past and hated them. Why should she revive their torment in the present? The war, she writes, "sits on me as a nightmare." But, like a nightmare, she shakes it off when she can.

Study? Ah, that alone is still real, as always. And she would have echoed the phrase that Sainte-Beuve loved, *On se lasse de tout excepté de comprendre.* "Thank Heaven," she says, "I led a lonely life of study in my youth and return to its rest with satisfaction." The books on her shelves are friends and companions who will not desert her. "When I am alive I hold audience with Plato, and when I am not, I gaze on his outside with delight." She learns Spanish by herself at seventy and reads Don Quixote with relish, complaining only that the pronunciation is impossible for her. Yet, after all, even books are but pale comforters, when life is behind instead of before. And in a dull, dark moment she confesses that she reads mainly to kill time.

As the years grow shorter and the hours longer, the one thing that she falls back upon more and more is the affections of home. Her memory fails her, her great mental powers no longer sustain her. But, in noting this, she observes with touching pathos, "I may be childish, but there are no limits to love." In her

active years she had never depended upon those around
her for comfort or for diversion.   To her sister-in-law,
who remarked that she was contented only when she
had all her children in the room with her, Mrs. Ripley
said that she did not require her children's presence so
long as she knew that they were happy.   But as time
flowed on, her heart turned more to the contact of those
she loved.   It pleased her to be busy for them, when she
could, though she deplored the weakness and ineptitude
of age in this regard.   "It seems strange that I that have
so litle to do, should do that little wrong."   It pleased her
to have them about her.   She writes to the daughter she
loved best, with winning tenderness: "I feel a want un-
satisfied, and I think it must be to see you.   Now this
is somewhat of a concession for one who has always
professed entire independence.   But there is often,
nowadays, a solitude of the heart which nothing can fill
except your image."

She loved to hear the prattle of her grandchildren, to
watch their pretty, wild activities, as if they were creatures of her dreams.   So they were, and she regarded
them, as she regarded the whole world and her own
soul, with a sad and gentle curiosity.   In such a tender
atmosphere of thought, of love, and of memory, she
faded away, in the spirit of the beautiful words which

she herself wrote not many weeks before the end: "We have kept step together through a long piece of road in the weary journey of life: we have loved the same beings and wept together over their graves. I have not your faith to console me, as they drop one after another from my side; yet my will, I trust, is in harmony with the divine order, and resigned where light is wanting. The sun looks brighter and my home more tranquil as the evening of life draws near."

III

Now, to consider Mrs. Ripley as she was in her best years, from thirty to sixty, with all her wealth of spiritual power and practical usefulness. We find, of course, the same qualities that we studied in her youth, but amplified, enriched, and balanced by the full development of maturity and a broader contact with the world.

And first, the wife and mother and housekeeper. It must be admitted that Mrs. Ripley's natural tastes did not lie in this direction. All the more notable is it that she was as admirable and successful here as in more abstract and ambitious pursuits. She herself recognizes amply that in giving up her cherished interests for a life of active usefulness she had found gain as well as loss.

"I once thought a solitary life the true one, and, contrary to my theory, was moved to give up the independence of an attic covered with books for the responsibilities and perplexities of a parish and a family. Yet I have never regretted the change. Though I have suffered much, yet I have enjoyed much and learned more." And housekeeping for her meant, not a ladylike supervision, but hard, perpetual labor. She rarely had a servant, she had many children, she had large social obligations, and for years she had the needs of a boys' school to provide for. Whatever her life lacked, it was not activity. The fret, the wear, the burden of all these cares she undoubtedly felt, especially as her health was never of the best. Sometimes she longed unutterably to be free and quiet. But she never complained, she never grew sour or querulous. Says one who knew her and loved her: "In all the annoyances of an overtaxed life I never saw her temper touched. She did not know resentment; she seemed always living in a sphere far above us all, yet in perfect sympathy."

As a wife and mother she did her full duty as if it were a pleasure. The affection, almost devotion, with which her husband speaks of her is sufficient evidence as to her relation to him. I have already said that she did not depend upon her children for amusement; but she watched over them and entered into their lives as only her intelligence could. Her methods of training and education were those of sympathy and kindness, and better testimony to their success could not be afforded than the noble qualities and eminent usefulness of her sons and daughters.

No account of these middle years of Mrs. Ripley's life would be complete without an analysis of her contact with the world, with her fellow men and women. In one way her career was an isolated, or at least a limited, one. She never traveled, knew nothing even of her own country outside the circle of her immediate surroundings. Books and talk, however, gave her a far wider knowledge of mankind than this would promise. And, though she did not go to the world, the world came to her. Her father's houses in Boston and Duxbury were always open to friends and neighbors, and during her husband's long ministration in his Waltham parish, she kept up a hospitality which never failed or weakened. All sorts of people were welcomed in her parlor, and if her thoughts were often called away to other higher or lower cares, she did not show it and her visitors never knew it.

This is not saying that her duties were not sometimes irksome. Occasionally, in her most intimate correspondence, she rebelled and uttered what she felt. "I would there were any hole to creep out of this most servile of all situations, a country clergyman's wife. Oh, the insupportable fatigue of affected sympathy with ordinary and vulgar minds." Yet an impatience like this was but momentary, and was in no way incompatible with the social charm which I have already indicated in Mrs. Ripley's youth, and which continued and increased with age. She certainly did not seek society, in fact preferred the multitudinous solitude of her own thoughts; but neither did she avoid her fellows, and when with them she had always the supreme attraction of being wholly and perfectly herself. There was no affectation, no convention in her manners or in her talk. She said what she thought, and, as her thoughts were wide, abundant, and original, her conversation could not fail to be stimulating. She was, indeed, more interested in the thoughts of others than in her own, and never permitted herself to be burdened with the demands of making talk where there was none.

The shyness of early years persisted in the form of quiet self-effacement. In the words of one who knew her well, "Without being precisely shy, she often gave one the impression of an unobtrusive, yet extreme solicitude to be in nobody's way." And this is not the worst of social qualities. It must not, however, in Mrs. Ripley's case, suggest dullness. When she did speak, it was with the ease and the fertility of a full soul. To Dr. Hedge it seemed that she had "an attraction proceeding from no personal charms, but due to the astonishing vivacity, the *all-aliveness,* of her presence, which made it impossible to imagine her otherwise than wideawake and active in word or work."

Yet even so, I have not quite portrayed the singular candor and impersonality of Mrs. Ripley's spirit. Her lower self did not exist for her; that is, she left it to regulate its doings by an exquisite instinct, without cumbering her soul with it. When her friends, in jest, engaged her in speculative talk and then put a broom in her hands and asked her to carry it across Boston Common, she did it quite without thought. In the same way, she carried her own external, social person through life, bearing it with the flawless and unfailing dignity that belonged to high preoccupations, and so making contact with her one of the privileges and delights of all she met.

Among the activities of Mrs. Ripley's prime none is more illustrative of her character than her teaching. She taught boys for many years, sometimes as an assistant in her husband's boarding-school, or again simply taking pupils to tutor in her own house. I find very little evidence that she enjoyed the work. Of course, there was the rare pleasure of really waking up a soul, knowing and seeing that you have done so. But the teacher was too self-distrustful to take much credit, even in such cases. She hated all responsibility — how much, then, the responsibility of a young life. She hated drudgery, of body or soul, though her whole long existence was made up of it. And whatever pleasure there may be in teaching, few will deny that there is drudgery also. Especially she hated discipline, believed at least that she had no faculty for it, and refused to practice it in any harsher sense. It is said that, as she sat in her teacher's chair, she knitted assiduously and purposely, so that small infractions of propriety might escape her notice. It is said, also, that when such things were forced upon her, she made no comment at the time, but afterwards wrote gentle, pleading notes to the culprits, which never failed of their effect.

For, whatever she may have felt herself, her pupils thought her eminently successful as a teacher. They learned from her, they obeyed her, they admired her, they loved her. No one affords better evidence than she that the stimulus of the soul goes further than the stim-

ulus of the rod. Most of her boys were rich, idle fellows,
who had been suspended from college or had never been
able to get there. Such hearts are not always bad, but
you have got to touch them to help them. On this point I
do not know that I can quote better testimony than that
of Senator Hoar. He says of the pupils who came to
her from college: "She would keep them along in all
their studies, in most cases better instructed than they
would have been if they had stayed in Cambridge. I
remember her now with the strongest feelings of rever-
ence, affection, and gratitude. In that I say only what
every other pupil of hers would say. I do not think she
ever knew how much her boys loved her."

I cannot leave Mrs. Ripley's teaching and practical
usefulness better than with the pathos of that last
sentence.

IV

THERE is no doubt that the chief interest of Mrs.
Ripley's best years, as of her youth, is in her intellectual
preoccupations. It is true that she theoretically sub-
ordinates such preoccupations to useful action, but her
very words in doing this show her attitude. "I sympathize much with your tranquil enjoyment in study.
There is no enjoyment like it, except perhaps disinter-

ested action; but all action is disturbing, because one is constantly limited and annoyed by others." So, in spite of the immense activity that was forced upon her by her choice of life and her surroundings, she persisted day after day and year after year in grasping more firmly and more zealously the things of the spirit.

Sometimes, indeed, the difficulties were so great that even her courage faltered. "I begin to think we must either live for earth *or* heaven, that there is no such thing as living for both at the same time."

Her health was uncertain; her time was broken, till there seemed nothing left of it; those about her would call her attention to petty details and trifling matters, world removed from the high thoughts she loved to linger with. It made no difference. The persistence — call it obstinacy — which others expended upon social success, upon worldly profit, upon mere immediate pleasure, she devoted wholly to books, to study, to vaster acquisition of varied knowledge; and somehow or other she knit up the flying minutes, which many would have wasted, into connected hours of profitable toil.

Note that this spiritual effort was given to intellectual interests pure and simple. Mrs. Ripley had never any great love for the æsthetic side of life. Music, unless as a matter of analytical study, made little appeal to her.

Art made almost none. "I am not sufficiently initiated into the mysteries of art to admire the right things," she says. Even in poetry her tastes were narrowly limited. The Classics she read because they were the Classics. To the moderns she gave little attention and less care. So with contemporary events. They passed her by almost unnoticed. Her whole thought was given to the eternal.

Note also that she did not study, to make a parade of it. She was as far as possible from a pedant in her speech as in her thought. She had no desire whatever to give instruction, simply to get it. Nor did literary ambition enter at all into her enthusiasm. She never wrote, had probably no great gift for formal writing. Her one inspiring passion, from youth to age, was to use every power she had in making just a little more progress into the vast, shadowy regions of obtainable knowledge.

As I have already pointed out in connection with her young days, her intellectual appetite was universal in its scope. It almost seemed as if she did not care upon what she used her mind, so long as she used it. The truth was, that every study was so delightful that choice was hardly necessary. Language? All languages fascinated her, and she grasped eagerly at every one that came within her reach. The ethereal flights of pure mathematics and astronomy might have absorbed her altogether, had it not been that chemistry and botany offered attractions so perpetually and variously alluring. The close contemporary of Thoreau, she had none of his imaginative interpretation of the natural world; but it is doubtful whether his actual knowledge of plants and trees was more exact than hers.

On the whole, it must be said, however, that her chief interest was in philosophy and abstract thought. The intense preoccupation with heaven and hell which beset every New England childhood in those days, turned, with her, as with so many others, into a close and keen analysis of where heaven and hell came from — and where they had gone to. She read the Greek and the English and the German philosophers and meditated upon them, with the result of a complete, profound, and all-involving intellectual scepticism. Observe that this scepticism was individual, not general. She was no dogmatic agnostic, no blatant unbeliever; above all, she abhorred the thought of leading any other astray. She was simply a humble, gentle, reverent seeker, ever anxious to know whether any one had found the light, but irrevocably determined to accept no false gleam, no deluding will-o'-the-wisp.

Even in face of the greatest mystery of all she would express only a deep resignation, making no pretense to a confidence she could not feel. "Death is an event as natural as birth, and faith makes it as full of promise. But faith is denied to certain minds, and submission must take its place. The Unknown, which lighted the morning of life, will hallow and make serene its evening. Conscious or unconscious, we shall rest in the lap of the Infinite. Enough of this. Let us live while we live, and snatch each fleeting moment of truth and love and beauty."

It may easily be maintained that Mrs. Ripley carried intellectual sincerity too far. She was so conscientious that she made a dogma, and finally even a duty, of doubt. She too often overlooked the blessed privilege of thorough scepticism, which is that it leaves hope as permissible as despair. Yet such singular, lucid, unfailing devotion to pure truth is highly notable in any one. I do not know whether a man may be forgiven for assuming that it is especially notable in a woman.

It is in this connection that I find a peculiar interest in Mrs. Ripley's intimacy with her nephew by marriage, — Emerson. It would seem as if the two must have been an infinite source of stimulus and solace to each other. That there was always the deepest affection and respect

between them is perfectly evident. When Mrs. Ripley
refers to Waldo in her earlier letters, it is as to a spirit
inspired and almost super-earthly. And in her old age
she writes of his absence, " I miss my guide and support
in many ways." Emerson's tone is no less enthusiastic,
not only in the eulogy of his friend, published soon after
her death, but in many passages of his " Journal."

Yet, with all this, one is rather surprised to note that
the two seem to see little of each other, do not seek in
each other's society that constant sympathy that one
would think they would have found there. The truth
is, their ways of looking at life were radically different.
Mrs. Ripley records a conversation between them in
which she remarked that "the soul's serenity was at
best nothing more than resignation to what could not be
helped"; and Emerson rejoined: "Oh, no, not resignation, aspiration is the soul's true state! What have we
knees for, what have we hands for? Peace is victory."

This difference of attitude peeps out slyly in a touch
here and there in Mrs. Ripley's letters. It is glaringly
marked in the study of her, printed at large in the sixth
volume of Emerson's " Journal." He does, indeed, repeat, with entire sincerity, much of his former praise.
But he adds these somewhat harsh comments: "She
would pardon any vice in another which did not obscure

his intellect or deform him as a companion. She knows perfectly well what is right and wrong, but it is not from conscience that she acts, but from sense of propriety, in the absence, too, of all motives to vice. She has not a profound mind, but her faculties are very muscular, and she is endowed with a certain restless and impatient temperament, which drives her to the pursuit of knowledge, not so much for the value of the knowledge, but for some rope to twist, some grist to her mill."

Few spiritual touches could be more instructive than this conflict of minds so akin in many interests and so closely thrown together. A certain justice in Emerson's complaints is undeniable. Mrs. Ripley's was in no way a creative, original intelligence. She knew that it was not, and perhaps we may say, did not wish it to be. Her mental activity does at times appear an effort at diversion and distraction, rather than a passionate struggle toward the ultimate ends of thought. Yet it is hard to be satisfied with Emerson's criticism, when one reads passages like the following: " Religion has become so simple a matter to me — a yearning after God, an earnest desire for the peace that flows from the consciousness of union with Him. It is the last thought that floats through my mind as I sleep, the first that comes when I wake. It forms the basis of my present life, saddened by past experience. It bedims my eyes with tears when I walk out into the beautiful nature where love is all around me. And yet no direct ray comes to my soul."

The true cause of the difference between Mrs. Ripley and Emerson was that her unconquerable, uncompromising dread of illusion did not suit his persistent and somewhat willful optimism. The lucid shafts of her penetrating intelligence drove right through his gorgeous cloud-fabric. Doubtless she listened to his golden visions with the profoundest attention and respect. But she was ten years older than he; she had known him as a boy and from boyhood, and she read the boy in the man and the angel, and he knew she did.

I have no direct evidence whatever, but I am inclined to suspect that she regarded those eager pages, peppered with capitalized abstractions, as Waldo's pretty playthings, which amused Waldo and could hurt nobody.

Emerson's verdict on Mrs. Ripley's moral character also, if not unjust, is misleading. It might naturally be expected that scepticism so complete would have some moral effects; but in this case those mainly perceptible are a divine gentleness and tolerance. Theoretical disbelief is apt to blight action. But action was so forced upon Mrs. Ripley all her life, that she could neither shun it nor neglect it. As to her moral instincts, Emerson himself indicates their sureness and delicacy. They never failed her in any connection. It was far more than a negative correctness of conduct. It was the most subtle and pervading sympathy with purity, holiness, and sacrifice, wherever they might be found. Above all, there was in her letters as in her life — and this Emerson fully recognizes — a singular tenderness, a pervading grace of comprehension, that endeared her to all who knew her. And hers is the saying, notable in one who so greatly prized all honesty and veracity. "The law of love is higher than the law of truth." In short, it may well be said that she believed in nothing but goodness, kindliness, the dignity of virtue and the unfailing delight of the pursuit of knowledge. Even as to these things she sometimes doubted, though they were clamped with iron tenacity to the inmost fiber of her soul, as to the existence of which she doubted also.

But, however great the charm of Mrs. Ripley's pure and saintly external life, the chief interest of her character, and of her example, must always lie in her extraordinary devotion to intellectual matters. It is to be observed that from her early childhood to her age this devotion was absolutely disinterested. Most men who make a business of study combine it with some ulterior object, either professional success, or financial profit, or the glory of literary achievement or of scientific discovery. This woman never entertained the slightest suggestion of such advantage. With her there was but one aim,— the pure exercise of thought for itself, the perpetual probing a little deeper and a little deeper and a little deeper into the vast, elusive mystery of existence. Such a tremendous and unceasing voyage of discovery carried its own triumph and its own satisfaction with it, and its resources of desire and delight were as varied as they were inexhaustible.

In Pater's "Imaginary Portrait," Sebastian van Storck says to his mother, "Good mother, there are duties towards the intellect also, which women can but rarely understand." No man ever understood those duties to the intellect better than this woman understood them.

III
MARY LYON

CHRONOLOGY

Mary Lyon

Born in Buckland, Massachusetts, February 28, 1797.
Mount Holyoke Seminary opened November, 1837.
Died March 5, 1849.

MARY LYON

III

MARY LYON

I

MARY LYON, the foundress of Mount Holyoke College, had a magnificently persistent spirit. She did what she set out to do and got what she wanted to get. No doubt the grit and determination in her were fostered, if not bred, by the sturdy, rugged training of her childhood. Born at the very close of the eighteenth century, on a farm in western Massachusetts, she was brought up by a widowed mother with many children and small means. The discipline was stern, but it rooted character deep down among the solid needs and essential efforts of existence. Every moment of life was of use and was put to use. When Mary was hardly out of infancy, her mother found her one day apparently trifling with the hourglass, but she explained that she thought she had discovered a way of making more time.[1] As years went on, she did make more time, by getting double work and thought into what there was. It was not time only; but every resource of life must be made to yield all there was in it and a little more.

"Economy," she said to her pupils later, "is not always doing without things. It is making them do the best they can." [2] Nothing helps so much towards this final extraction of utility as knowing the exact nature of things, not only what they serve for, but how they are made, even knowing how to make them one's self. Mary made her own clothes from cloth made by her own hands. Many other women did this; but Mary, when she lived near a brickyard, wanted to make brick, and did it. Always she had the instinct and the habit and the genius for doing something.

Very early, however, she appreciated that to do something, in her sense, a wider and ampler education was needed than a New England farm would give her. The most essential education — that of character — she could indeed give herself. Self-training, self-discipline, she began early and kept up to the end. When a friend ventured to suggest the getting rid of certain little awkwardnesses, she replied, with perfect good humor, "I have corrected more such things than anybody ought to have." [3] She corrected little defects as well as great.

But no one knew better than she that education could not come wholly from within. There were broad regions of spiritual joy and spiritual usefulness which must be explored by the help and the guidance of others.

The means of obtaining such help and guidance for women in those days were limited, and Mary's situation and circumstances made them doubly limited for her. But what persistent and determined effort could do, she did. Her natural capacity for acquisition was undoubtedly great. She said of herself, in a connection that precluded boasting, "My mind runs like lightning."[4] It not only moved swiftly, but it held what it seized as it went. She was given a Latin grammar on Friday night. On Monday she recited the whole of it. I do not know how much this means, not having seen the grammar; but obviously it means enough, even with her humiliating confession that she had studied all day Sunday.

In her case, however, it was less the brilliancy than the everlasting persistence that counted. She had no money to get an education. Very well, she would get the money first and the education afterward. She went to school when she could; when she could not, she taught others — for seventy-five cents a week and her board. The opportunities that she did get for her own work she improved mightily. Those with whom she boarded when she was studying say that she slept only four hours out of the twenty-four. They add, with the amazement which persons differently constituted feel for such endeavor: "She is all intellect: she does not know that she has a body to care for." [5]

But do not imagine that she was a mere human machine, created to think of work only. She had her ups and downs, as those who sleep only four hours must —her days when work seemed impossible and, what is worse, not worth doing; her utter discouragements, when the only relief was tears. She inquired one night how soon tea would be ready; was told, immediately; and on being asked the reason of her evident disappointment, replied: "I was only wishing to have a good crying-spell, and you could not give me time enough." [6]

How far other emotions touched her active youth we do not know. She was always sweet and merry with her companions, but she had not leisure for much social dissipation. One or two vague glimpses come of loving or, much more, of being loved, but they lead to nothing. Other interests more absorbing filled that eager and busy heart. As she looked back from later triumphs at the struggles of these early days, she said: "In my youth I had much vigor — was always aspiring after something. I called it loving to study. Had few to direct me aright. One teacher I shall always remember. He told me education was to fit one to do good." [7]

Whatever education might be, she sought it with a fervent zeal which was an end in itself as well as a most efficient means.

II

To get an education for herself, with heroic effort, was not enough for Miss Lyon. In getting it, she came to feel its value and others' need of it. Obtaining it for them was an object for as much zeal and devotion as she had bestowed upon her own. No one then felt it necessary that women should be educated as men were. Men, whether educated themselves or not, felt it to be distinctly unnecessary; and the suggestion of systematic intellectual training for the weaker, domestic sex did not fill the ordinary husband and father with enthusiasm. A fashionable finishing school was a girl's highest ambition, and to be accomplished, pending being married, was the chief aim of her existence. To Miss Lyon it seemed that women had brains as well as men, were as well able to use them, and often more eager. And she determined very early to devote her life to giving them the opportunity.

Her object was certainly not money-making. Her personal standards were always simple, and her earnings, when she did earn, would seem, even to the modern teacher, pitiful. In fact, her view of profit and the teacher's profession, like that of Socrates, was ideal to the point of extravagance. "If money-making is your object," she cries, "be milliners or dressmakers; but teaching is a sacred, not a mercenary employment."[8]

So with the ambition to be great and prominent and remembered. Who shall say that any one is wholly free from the subtle and searching temptation here? But at least she is free from it so far as she knows herself. Some, she writes, will say that Miss Grant and Miss Lyon wish to have "a great institution established, and to see themselves at the head of the whole, and then they will be satisfied."[9] And she recognizes that this is human nature, and she does not trouble herself to deny the allegation directly, but her tone implies that it touches her not.

Nor did she seek to be of use to those who had wealth or social prominence or influence. They could take care of themselves. What she wished to provide for was the great mass of women throughout the country who had little means or none, but the same devouring thirst for better things that had tormented her. She would exclude no one who was really worthy, no one, as she said herself, but "harmless cumberers of the ground" and those "whose highest ambition is to be qualified to amuse a friend in a vacant hour." [10] Such, rich or poor, might find their vocation elsewhere. The saving of their souls was not her business.

So, trusting in the goodness of God and in her own unbounded energy, she set about taking a great step in the forward progress of the world. She was practically unknown; she had no money; she had no influence, she had no access to the many agencies which facilitate the advancement of great undertakings. She had only courage and hope. "When we decide that it is best to perform a certain duty, we should expect success in it, if it is not utterly impossible," [11] she said quietly; and she practiced as she preached. She was ready to make any sacrifice. "Our personal comforts are delightful, not essential." [12]

She approached every one who could possibly help her, with tireless, but not tedious, persistency. She went into people's homes and pointed out what she was trying to do for them, showed fathers and mothers what their daughters needed and how little effort would help to get it.

She spoke publicly on formal occasions; she spoke privately to any one who she thought might assist her, even to strangers. Some of her friends complained of this. In that day it seemed odd for a woman to make herself so conspicuous, and the doubters feared that she might injure her cause instead of aiding it. She differed from them positively. "What do I do that is wrong?" she urged. "I hope I behave like a lady; I mean to do so." Who that knows anything of her will question that she did? But she was working for a great cause and she did not mean to let trifles stand in her way. "My heart is sick," she cried; "my soul is pained with this empty gentility, this genteel nothingness. I am doing a great work. I cannot come down."[13]

Of course there were discouragements, crying spells, no doubt, as in the earlier days; times when everything went wrong, and the world seemed utterly indifferent. The very vastness of the hope made it shadowy, and she had her lurking possibilities of scepticism. "I always fear when I find my heart thus clinging to the hope of future good."[14] There was physical collapse, too, under such enormous effort, even in a body mainly healthy. For two or three days, sometimes, she would give herself up to a state of partial stupor, forgetting even hope and duty in an absolute relaxation of all nervous energy.

Then she would emerge, with fatigue and depression behind her, ready to face any difficulty and overcome any obstacle. "It is one of the nicest of mental operations," she said, "to distinguish between what is very difficult and what is utterly impossible." [15] But what was impossible to others was apparently only difficult to her. Walls hardly built and hardly paid for might fall down, and her only comment was one of delight that no one was hurt. Stupid and obstinate people might oppose her methods, but somehow or other she accomplished the result. "She made the impression on every one with whom she had anything to do, from the common day-laborer to the president of a college, that if she set herself to do anything, it was of no use to oppose her." [16]

This does not mean that she was rough or overbearing in her methods, that she forced money out of pockets, or souls into the kingdom of God. She had, indeed, her share of the prophet's severity. If she had let herself go, she might have reprehended and reprimanded with a righteous scorn. In one wealthy household, where she had expected much, she got nothing, and to friends who had foretold her failure she confided, with bitterness: "They live in a costly house; it is full of costly things; they wear costly clothes, but oh, they're little bits of folks!" [17]

Such bitterness she mainly kept to herself, however. She knew that her progress must be slow, often hindered, and often tortuous. She disciplined herself not to hope too much and to forget disappointments. She practiced infinite patience. "I learned twenty years ago never to get out of patience."[18] She would not dispute or argue. She would state her position, her plans, her prospects. She would answer every question which really tended to clarify. Then the conscience of her hearers was left to work by itself. Attacks, abuse, sarcasm, slander, touched her not. She did not deserve them, why should she heed them? They distressed her friends, and one of the closest, Professor Hitchcock, wrote an answer which he submitted to Miss Lyon's consideration. "That was the last I ever saw of it," he said.[19]

Instead of this sharper combativeness, she worked by persuasion, by insinuation, by tact and sympathy. She would not yield a syllable of her main theory; but if anything was to be gained by meeting criticism in a detail, by accepting a minor suggestion, she was always ready. "In deviating from others," she advised, "be as inoffensive as possible; excite no needless opposition"[20] She excited none, where it could be avoided, and people found themselves agreeing with her before they knew it, and almost against their will. She conquered less by formal argument than by personal charm, and had the golden faculty of making others feel that her will was their own. One who knew her well said that she held men "by invisible attractions which it was hard to resist and from which very few wished to be released."[21] Another simpler mind put it still better: "I would have done anything she asked me to. Everybody would."[22]

The habit of getting what she wanted from others came naturally. That of making use of what she got, perhaps somewhat less so. She had to train herself a little in business methods. This a clear and sound brain can always do, and she did it. But order and system and punctuality seem at first to have been difficult for her. She was not born neat and tidy in trifles. Some women's things, she said, seemed to have feet and to know their right places and return to them of their own accord. Hers did not. She was not born punctual or with a consciousness of time. If she got interested in a task, she wanted to finish it, regardless of the arrival of the hour for doing something else. She wanted to go to bed when she pleased, to get up when she pleased; not at a set and given minute.

But she understood these weaknesses, and had conquered them in all essentials, before she entered upon her great work. If she was not born a woman of business, she made herself one, and she had overcome inner obstacles before she began her fight with those without. Therefore she was able, not only to raise the sums she needed, but to use them wisely; and, after innumerable difficulties, in the autumn of 1837, Mount Holyoke Seminary was opened.

It was a day of triumph for Miss Lyon — of pure, personal triumph, of course it was. She would not have been human if it had not been. She had labored through years of toil and vexation. Now at last the way was clear to accomplish what she had dreamed. Of an earlier time of prosperity she says: "There is an unusual evenness and uniformity in my feelings, freedom from excitement, or any rising above the common level." [23] But on that November day in 1837 her spirits certainly did rise above the common level. She saw all that she had longed for and hoped for realized in that plain, square building with its vast possibilities, and her words have the inspiration of a prophetess: "The stones and brick and mortar speak a language which vibrates through my very soul." [24]

III

So she had performed her huge task, her practically single-handed task, of preparing the material facilities for extending education. Now came the subtle and complicated labor of conveying it. And first as to the negative problem, so to speak, that of discipline. This considerable body of girls had been brought together, unaccustomed to the restraints of community life. How to train them to do their best work without injuring themselves or each other?

To begin with, Miss Lyon did not believe too much in formal rules. Of course a certain number of such rules was necessary, as always. But she endeavored to impress upon her girls the spirit of those rules and not the letter. She brought home to them vividly the struggle between the body and the mind, and the absolute necessity of making the mind master at the start. "The mind," she told them, "should not sit down and wash the body's feet, but the body should obey the mind." [25]

So in relations with others. It was not so much a question of following rules as of getting into the right tone. "Avoid trying the patience or irritating the feelings of others," [26] she reminded them. She made her precise directions flow from such general precepts as these.

Then she trusted the girls to carry them out. Of course, they could not always be trusted, and she knew that they could not. They were human and young and

girls, and had their weaknesses. Dress and boys were
in their thoughts, as they always have been and always
will be. But something about Miss Lyon's presence
took the place of rules — something about the thought
of her presence. "One could not do wrong where she
was," [27] writes one pupil. There were occasionally those
who could do wrong and did, either from carelessness
or even from contumacy. With them Miss Lyon had
such vigor as was needed. Read the quaint old biographer's account of the forcible removal of one young
woman from one room to another: "'You *must* go into
the large room,' said the teacher." The young woman
went.[28]

But usually the reliance was less upon coercion than
upon persuasion. "She will try to make us vote so-
and-so, and I won't vote that way — I won't," [29] said one
recalcitrant to another as they prepared to listen to her
gentle exhortation. Then they voted as she wished.
Above all, her discipline was dynamic, consisted in instill-
ing a bewitching impluse to do things, not to avoid things.
"Our happiness lies largely in remembering," she said;
"do what will be pleasant to remember." And whatever you do, put life into it. Do not half do, or do
negligently. "Learn to sit with energy." [30] Did ever
any one put more character into a phrase than that?

And as they were taught energy, so they were taught the use of it by order and method. Hours should be planned and kept and followed. "I have suffered all my life from the want of regular habits," she told her girls; "I wish you to accustom yourselves to be thoroughly systematic in the division of your time and duties." [31] Train and discipline the mind, she urged upon them, govern your thoughts. "Bring the mind to a perfect abstraction and let thought after thought pass through it." [32]

She herself was ardent, full of emotion, full of impulse. "I endeavor daily to avoid excessive emotions on any subject," [33] she says. She was not always successful, and admitted it; but she wanted those who learned from her to be better than she. Even in giving, in charity, which meant so much to her, she advised restraint and intelligence. "If you had really rather spend your money on yourselves, spend it." Do not overdo from the impulse of the moment. "I don't want artificial fire." [34] In short, she was as anxious to make progress solid and sure as to establish it upon an undying enthusiasm. "Character," she told those incorrigible workers of samplers, "like embroidery, is made stitch by stitch." [35]

From all this you gather perhaps an impression of

pedantry, of formal priggishness. It is true that, as we look back from the familiarity of to-day, Miss Lyon's methods and manners sometimes seem stiff, like her caps. Her girls to her were always "young ladies," as their contemporaries of the other sex were "young gentlemen." Her phraseology was elaborate, and she wished others to use the same. In her portraits one perceives a certain primness, and the undeniable beauty has also an undeniable suggestion of austerity. If haste made her sometimes forget to fasten a button or adjust a tie, one imagines her upon any state occasion as complete in her dignity as Queen Elizabeth herself.

But brief study suffices to penetrate beneath this superficial stiffness and form. "It is very important a teacher should not be schoolified," [36] said Miss Lyon to her pupils.

Many teachers say this, not so many practice it. She did. Under the formal garb and manner, she was essentially human. In the first place, she had the keenest insight into human strength and weakness. She knew the heart, or at least knew that none of us know it, and was ever alive to opportunities to increase her knowledge. In one case she comments with the keenest analysis upon the weaknesses of a relative, and then apologizes for doing so; "only I love to remark the

extreme unlikeness in members of the same family." [37]
In general, the good qualities impress her most, though
she notes this with due reserve: "On the whole, as I
grow in years, I have a better opinion of people." [38]

But her humanity went far deeper than mere observation and insight. Under the formal outside there was
the most sensitive affection and tenderness. She loved
her pupils as if they were her daughters, felt as if she
must supply the mother's place to every one of them.

"You are spoiling that child," said her teachers, of
one whom she petted, though she never really showed
any favoritism. Her answer was: "Well, she is young
and far from her mother, and I am sorry for her, and
I don't believe it will hurt her." [39]

This was only one instance out of many. When girls
were solitary and homesick and weary and discouraged, she could and did sympathize, for she had known
all those things herself and went back readily to the
days when she had said that she had "but just physical
strength enough left to bear her home, just intellect
enough to think the very small thoughts of a little
infant, and just emotion enough to tremble under the
shock." [40]

In short, she had the supreme element of sympathy,
the power of always putting one's self in the place of

another.   Nothing can be of greater help to a teacher
or to any leader of men or women than this, and saying
after saying of Miss Lyon's shows how richly she was
endowed with it.   The brief remarks and comments
gathered at the end of Miss Fidelia Fiske's quaint little
volume of "Recollections" are the best illustration of
what I mean.   "More than nine tenths of the suffering
we endure is because those around us do not show that
regard for us which we think they ought to." [41]   This
bit of wisdom, curiously exaggerated for a thinker so
careful as Miss Lyon, is as interesting for what it suggests about herself as about her study and comprehension of others.

With the sympathetic and imaginative power of putting one's self in the place of others is apt to go a large
and fine sense of humor.   Had Miss Lyon this?   It is
amusing to see how answers vary.   Some of the numerous pupils who have written reminiscences of her insist
that she had no humor at all, that she rarely, if ever,
smiled, and took life always from the serious side.
Others are equally positive that she was ready for a
jest, and on occasion could twinkle with merriment.
The explanation of these conflicting views probably is
that she was very different with different people.   Some
persons have the faculty of cherishing the warm flame

of humor, of teasing even fretted spirits into bright and gracious gayety. Others put out that pleasant flame as a snuffer puts out a candle. I have known pupils of Miss Lyon with whom I am sure that she was always as serious as the bird of Pallas.

Then, too, she was brought up in an age that restrained laughter. As a teacher, she knew the danger of satire, and herself admitted that she had to be on her guard against her appreciation of the ludicrous, lest she should do irreparable damage to sensitive hearts. Moreover, the Puritan strain was strong in her and she shied at any suggestion of uncontrolled gayety for herself or those she guided. "It is not true," insists an admiring pupil, "that Miss Lyon enjoyed *fun!* . . . 'Fun,' she said, 'is a word no young lady should use.'" [42]

Yet I dare swear that she enjoyed fun just the same; that she could see a joke, and take and make a joke. One would certainly not say of her, in the dainty phrase of the old poet, —

> "Her heart was full of jigs and her feet did wander
>   Even as autumn's dust."

But, at any rate in youth, before care settled too heavily, she was capable of full-lunged, resounding cachinnation. "Mr. Pomeroy's father has heard Miss Lyon, when a girl, laugh half a mile away, from one

hill to another. Once she laughed so loud she scared
the colts in the field and made them run away." [43]

Now, isn't that jolly? In later years she did not,
indeed, scare the colts or the coltish young ladies, but
there can be no doubt that large possibilities of spiritual
laughter lightened the troubles and vexations that
were inseparable from her triumph. To be sure, she
sometimes fell into strange freaks of professional solemnity, such as seem quite inconsistent with any sense
of humor at all, as when she cautioned her young
ladies: "The violation of the seventh commandment
may and ought to be examined as a general subject,
but beware of learning particulars"; [44] or again:
"Choose the society of such gentlemen as will converse
without even once seeming to think that you are a
lady." [45] But I believe the winking of an eye would
have made her see the humorous slant of these suggestions. She saw it in regard to many others, and
especially in regard to that most delicate of humorous
tests, the absurdity of one's self. Is there not a depth
of humor in her overheard remark, as she stood before
the mirror trying to tie her bonnet-strings: "Well, I
may fail of heaven, but I shall be very much disappointed if I do—very much disappointed." [46]

All this analysis of Miss Lyon's educational influ-

ence, her discipline, her method, her sympathy, her
laughter, does not catch the entire depth and power
of it. We must add the magnetism, the gift of inspiration. She could draw money out of men's pockets; she
could draw folly out of girls' souls and put thought
and earnest effort in its place. Never give up, she
taught them; never submit, never be beaten. "Teach
till you make a success of it." [47] Live with high ideas,
she taught them; make noble dreams noble realities.
"Our thoughts have the same effect on us as the company we keep." [48] When you have a great object in
view, let no obstacle, no difficulty, distract you from it.
"Go where no one else is willing to go; do what no one
else is willing to do." [49]

And she herself never forgot the greatest test of
teaching; did her best to keep it before all who assisted
her and worked under her. "Make the dull ones think
once a day, make their eyes sparkle once a day." [50] The
teacher who can do this has indeed magnetism, has inspiration. She did it, perhaps many times a day.

IV

It is interesting that the enthusiasm of scholarship
proper is not a marked element in Miss Lyon. She
had an immense desire to educate herself; later, an im-

mense desire to educate others. It does not appear
that in youth or in age she was overpowered by the
passion for acquiring knowledge as an end merely.
Now and then she has words that seem to belie this.
"There are peculiar sweets derived from gaining knowledge, delights known only to those who have tested
them,"[51] she says. She pursued all varieties of study
with equal ardor. Mathematics, logic, science, literature,—she was at home in all, delighted to talk about
them, delighted to teach them. But you feel instantly
the difference between her and, for example, Mrs.
Samuel Ripley, in this regard. Mrs. Ripley followed
all studies because they were all in themselves equally
delightful. Miss Lyon followed them all because they
were all, comparatively speaking, indifferent. To Mrs.
Ripley knowledge was an end in itself, an all-sufficing,
inexhaustible end. To Miss Lyon knowledge was only
a beginning. Mathematics and all the rest were bright,
sharp, splendid instruments. The first thing was to get
them; but an infinitely more important thing was what
you could do with them. What a significant, if uninten-
tional, revelation there is in the phrase I have already
quoted (italics mine): "In my youth I had much vigor
—was always aspiring after something. *I called it
loving to study.*"[52] What scorn there is in another

brief phrase of her later years: "The intellectual miser is an object of contempt." [53]

No, she was not essentially a scholar; she could never have been content to spend long hours and long years over books and the problems of books. She was essentially and by every instinct a teacher. And her object in teaching was not to make other scholars. In all the great volume of "Reminiscences" contributed by her pupils, pure scholarship fills but a very little place. What she aimed at was to teach girls, not to know, but to live. It is true, her biographer says that in her early years of teaching her great aim was to make scholars. But even so, I think she was anxious rather to succeed in anything she had undertaken than to impart the fine fury of intellectual acquirement.

And as time went on, the mere lore of books took a more and more subordinate place. Life was to be studied, character was to be studied, all the curious, subtle, surrounding and moulding influences that govern our existence. "Make as much effort to gain knowledge from objects around us, from passing events, and from conversation, as from books." [54] She labored hard and long at the greatest of human tasks, — that of making people think for themselves. "Knowledge and reflection," she said, "should balance"; — though she added, with a sigh, that "all we can do in this matter, is to stand about the outer court and say, 'Won't you reflect?'"[55]

And her object was not only reflection, but reflection turned into conduct. She wanted to take a group of bright and eager spirits from the great middle circle of democracy and send them out again to make over the world. This America, as she then saw with almost prophetic vision, needed so many things, some consciously and some unconsciously. She wanted her girls to do something toward supplying the need. "We have made it an object," she said, "to gain enlarged and correct views . . . as to what needs to be done, what can be done, what ought to be done; and, finally, as to what is our duty."[56]

To know one's duty, in the largest sense, and to do it, was her idea of education. As one of her pupils expresses it, "her first aim was to make us Christians; her second to cultivate us intellectually."[57] But her own phrase, far finer, rings like a trumpet: "That they should live for God and do something."[58]

V

HERE we have the essence of Miss Lyon's teaching, of her work in the world, of her own heart, — that they should live for God and do something. Is it not, so far as it goes, a splendid, direct, and simple clue to the great problem of education? It is, perhaps, for the lack of such a clue that nowadays we grope and flounder so dismally. For who will deny that in all the difficulties that beset educative theory at the present day the greatest is that we do not know what we want? The old convenient standard of a liberal education is slipping from us, has slipped from us completely. What are we to put in the place of it? Two at least of our great institutions of learning have mottoes that suggest Miss Lyon's, "Not to be ministered unto but to minister," and "For Christ and the Church." But we can neither agree about what they mean nor unite to apply them. As with the unhappily married couple in Mr. Ade's Fable, "The motto in the dining-room said, 'Love one another,' but they were too busy to read." Instead, we turn to the practical issue of bread and butter, and make it our educational ideal to train men and women to go out into the world and contend with their fellows for the material necessaries of life.

Miss Lyon's aim was simpler — not always easy to apply, perhaps, but tangible, and, above all, inspiring from its very nature: That they should live for God and do something. But to understand the full bearing of the words, we must consider more carefully what God was to Miss Lyon herself.

To begin with, her religion was not a matter of convention, not a mere tradition accepted from others and passed on to others again, without an intimate grasp of its nature and meaning. She came slowly to the fullness and ripeness of faith; regretted often in her early years that the divine ecstasy descended less amply upon her than upon some more favored. She abhorred pretense, the theory of feeling; wanted only sentiments that were truly hers. How admirable is her confusion in the presence of great natural beauty: "I feared that I should be unable to feel the soul-moving power, and I had an ardent desire that I might not acknowledge, even to myself, any second-hand emotions, any influence which did not affect my own heart."[59] Second-hand emotions! Do we not all of us need to beware of them?

As religion took fuller possession of her, she did not suffer herself to be unduly exalted. To others it seemed to come with ease and swiftness of glory. It came with struggle and effort and long agony to her. "In view of invisible and divine realities, my mind is darkened, my preceptions feeble, my heart cold and stupid. It seems as if such a low, groveling worm of

the dust could never be fitted for heaven."[60] There
were days of distress and discouragement, days of bar-
renness, if not of doubt. "Sometimes I almost *feel*
that I am not my own, but I find my heart repeatedly
desiring those things from which I had almost supposed it was forever separated."[61]

A clear, calm, intellectual analysis was so natural to
her that she was tempted to apply it where faith and
love would have been more wholesome; although, in
the end, with the author of the "Imitation," she finds
that "after winter comes summer, after the night the
day, and after a storm a great calm." "It is wonderful to me how the mind, after a state of doubt
and difficulty from which it seemed impossible to be
extricated, can, without any new light or new evidence, settle down into a state of calm and quiet
decision."[62]

But all these negative elements were as nothing to
the joy and rapture which religion gave her. She was
certainly not a mystic in the sense of pure contempla-
tion. Action was life to her, her soul was dynamic,
and her conception of God must have been that of a
full, outflowing, energetic, creative love. But this energy of action came to her, seasoned and flavored with
rapturous delight. "I love sometimes," she says, "to

lose sight of individuals, in thinking of the bundles of eternal life and happiness that are bound up together in heaven." [63] And again: "But amidst the darkness, and with a burden on my heart which I cannot describe, there is something in my soul which seems like trust in God, that is like a peaceful river, overflowing all its banks." [64]

She wanted to bathe all who followed her in this peaceful river, to make them partakers of this sustaining and enduring joy; and to do this, she wanted to build up their souls on an assured and stable foundation of thought and devotion and self-control and self-sacrifice. It must be admitted that some of her methods for accomplishing her end seem to us now strange and a little repellent, though perhaps they were none the worse for that. Even to-day some persons feel that dancing is not a very profitable employment; but few would go so far as Miss Lyon: "When Satan would spread his net to fascinate, allure, and destroy, he never omits the dance." [65] The payment of small debts is undoubtedly desirable; but it is making a serious matter of it to urge that "it might be impossible, when praying for some one, to keep out of mind a ten cents her due." [66] Again, the following injunction seems a little portentous, though eminently appropriate to much modern youthful reading: "Never read a book without first praying over it." [67]

These extremes make us smile. Others more solemn make us tremble. Miss Lyon believed in hell with all her soul. "If she had ever a flitting doubt of the certainty of future retributions, that doubt was never known or suspected by her most intimate friends." [68] She proposed to have her pupils believe in hell also. She stood before them in chapel, a quiet, prim New England lady, and made hell real. "It was the warning voice of one who saw the yawning gulf. She would point to the dark, shelving, fatal precipice, without a gesture, without a motion, save of her moving lips, her hand laid devoutly on that well-worn octavo Bible. She would uncover the fiery billows rolling below, in the natural but low, deep tones with which men talk of their wills, their coffins, and their graves." [69] And this to a company of young girls, at the most sensitive, emotional age, just snatched from their sheltering homes and already unhinged by novel strains of every kind. It seems to us like saving their souls at fearful peril to their bodies.

Even Miss Lyon's most concrete definition of education, so often quoted, will hardly be quoted by any one to-day without a smile of good-natured amusement,—

"A lady should be so educated that she can go as a missionary at a fortnight's notice." [70]

Yet, in spite of all these excesses, I believe that the essence of the matter was with Miss Lyon. The minor drawbacks, the superficial eccentricities, — even hell, — fall away, and leave her dominant and vital with the supreme object of all her thought and life, which was God. Those who followed her, she taught, must get out of themselves, forget themselves: "How much happier you would be to live in a thousand lives beside yourself rather than to live in yourself alone!" [71] They must be ready to give all, to sacrifice all, to endure all, for Christ and His Kingdom: "Property, education, time, influence, friends, children, brothers and sisters, all should be devoted to this object!" [72] And in giving, in sacrificing, there should be no waywardness, no willfulness, no whim of the individual. "Neither teachers nor scholars should have any way of their own, or will of their own, but all should be swallowed up in the will of God." [73]

Finally, the heart of the whole was not merely doing, not merely the devoted, unremitting effort to do right, but rapture and glory: "Our minds are so constituted that nothing but God can fill them." [74]

"There is but one thing needful," said Amiel, "to

possess God." Miss Lyon thought it needful, not only to possess God herself, but to make all others possess Him, and she could not feel her own possession perfect when she was not laboring at this magnificent, if impossible, task.

IV

HARRIET BEECHER STOWE

CHRONOLOGY

Harriet Elizabeth Beecher.
Born in Litchfield, Connecticut, June 14, 1811.
At school in Hartford, 1824.
Converted, 1825.
Taught at Hartford, 1827 to 1832.
Went to Cincinnati, Ohio, to teach, 1832.
Married Rev. Calvin E. Stowe, January 6, 1836.
Removed to Brunswick, Maine, 1850.
"Uncle Tom's Cabin" published, 1852.
Removed to Andover, Massachusetts, 1852.
In Europe, 1853, 1856, 1859.
Removed to Hartford, 1863.
Mr. Stowe died August, 1886.
Died, July 1, 1896.

HARRIET BEECHER STOWE

IV
HARRIET BEECHER STOWE
I

SHE was a little woman, rather plain than beautiful, but with energy, sparkle, and vivacity written all over her. I always think of her curls, but they were not curls of coquetry or curls of sentiment; they were just alive, as she was, and danced and quivered when she nodded and glowed.

The first half of the nineteeth century, when she was growing up, was still the age of ministers in New England, and she was of a ministerial family, grew up in that atmosphere, and inherited all its traditions. Only she preached in books, not from the pulpit. She passed her youth among the joys and torments of religion, as then practiced. She married and had children. Then she set the world afire with "Uncle Tom's Cabin," made money, which she sorely needed, wrote more books, a huge number of them, made more money in proportion, spent it with much generosity and some joy, and died, perhaps a great author, certainly having been a great power in her day.

She did all this with health that was never robust, never reliable, and often wretched. " A wisp of nerve," [1] she calls herself; and she was. " She loved more," says her biographer, "and consequently suffered more than others, and the weight of her suffering was heavier because she had grown up, apparently, almost without care, either from herself or others, in behalf of her body." [2]   There were no gymnasiums for girls in those days, no vigorous outdoor sports, no lithe, swaying figures and red cheeks; only samplers and prayer. Mrs. Stowe often analyzed these conditions in her characters, and also analyzed them, with much acuteness, in herself.   "About half of my time I am scarcely alive, and a great part of the rest, the slave and sport of morbid feeling and unreasonable prejudice.   I have everything but good health." [3]

But do not suppose that she let morbid fancies or cringing nerves interfere when there was work to be done.   That generation had its weaknesses, and sometimes cultivated them; but it could trample on them, when occasion demanded, and even forget them.   Mrs. Stowe was an excellent manager, careful of her household, careful of her husband, careful of her children. She could be up early and down late, sew, clean, and cook, plan and provide.   When moving had to be attended to, she bore the burden. What that means, every housekeeper knows.

She appreciated the importance of order and system in a family: "I know that nothing can be done without it; it is the keystone, the *sine qua non,* and in regard to my children I place it next to piety."[4] She gives an amusing picture of her efforts to apply this principle in establishing a new home: furniture men flying about, servants calling, assistants suggesting, everything to be done, and nobody ready to do it.[5] Nerves were evidently out of place in such a scene as this, and she whipped them into submission — could even make fun when, in the midst of it, she received from her husband a letter, saturated with gloom, warning her that he could not live long, wondering what she could do as a widow, and urging prudence, as she would not have much to live on. Prudence! With big freight-bills to pay and the children clamoring for steak to sustain them through their labors!

When these whirlwinds of achievement are over, the nerves revenge themselves. Nerves usually do. She has times of depression so deep that she hardly seems to live: "All I wanted was to get home and die. Die I was very sure I should, at any rate, but I suppose I was never less prepared to do so."[6] Again, "I let my plants die by inches before my eyes, and do not water them, and I dread everything I do, and wish it was not to be done." [7] Yet, even in these depths, if there is a call from others in greater misery, she can respond, sometimes with soothing tenderness, sometimes with cheerful rallying. When her husband writes to her in utter despair, the sympathy of her answer is disguised in gentle mockery. "My dear Soul, I received your most melancholy effusion, and I am sorry to find it's just so. I entirely agree and sympathize. Why didn't you engage the two tombstones — one for you and one for me?" [8]

This gayety, which she could apply to her own troubles, of course made her delightful to others, and socially she was popular and much sought after. Like most persons of sensitive temperament and nervous organization, she at once liked society and shunned it. The instinct of avoiding people, of remaining shut up within herself, was strong in her, and she had to make an effort to overcome it: "I am trying to cultivate a general spirit of kindliness towards everybody. Instead of shrinking into a corner to notice how other people behave, I am holding out my hand to the right and to the left, and forming casual or incidental acquaintances with all who will be acquainted with me." [9] She cultivates the habit of speaking to disagreeable people, to nonentities, and finding the good that can surely be found in them. Also, she feels the intense excitement of social intercourse, with its consequent fatigue and reaction: "I believe it would kill me dead to live long in the way I have been doing since I have been here. It is a sort of agreeable delirium."[10]

In the main she likes people. Instead of saying, with Madame de Staal-Delaunay, that she is always glad to make new friends because she knows they cannot be worse than the old, she declares that she leaves Brunswick with regret, because she shall never find friends whom she likes better than those she has made there.

And men and women liked her, because she liked them. She entered many circles and mingled with all sorts of people, and everywhere she was received with esteem and affection. She herself speaks of the singular charm and fascination of her brother, Henry Ward Beecher: "He has something magnetic about him that makes everybody crave his society — that makes men follow and worship him."[11] The magnetism in her case was by no means so marked; but it was there, and very many found it irresistible.

If she was popular in general society and was liked by others because she liked them, much more had she a tender and devoted affection in the most intimate relations of life. "There is a heaven," she says, "a heaven — a world of love, and love after all is the life-blood, the existence, the all in all of mind." [12]   And in a simpler and even more penetrating phrase, she shows how thoroughly she had experienced what she estimates so highly: "Oh, Mary, we never know how we love till we try to unlove." [13]

Her devotion to her father and to her brothers and sisters was constant and unfailing. Perhaps the nearest of them all to her was Henry Ward Beecher, and the strength of her love for him appears strikingly in the letters written in regard to his greatest trial. She not only rejects all possible doubt as to his innocence and purity, but rejects it with a whole-hearted conviction which it is difficult to resist. He is herself, she says, and she feels a blow at him more than she would feel it at herself.

Her children she loved and tended and cared for, entering into all the interests of their lives and being prostrated by their illness or death. It certainly could not be said of her that she was a writer before she was a mother: "My children I would not change for all the ease, leisure, and pleasure that I could have without them." [14] Like all persons of deep and sensitive natures, she feels the utmost difficulty in expressing affection. What are those strange, those insurmountable barriers that make it impossible for the tenderness that fills our hearts to overflow our lips, so that we meet our dearest with a jest, or a quip, or a casual comment, instead of the sincere outpouring of passionate devotion? How many of us can echo Mrs. Stowe's words: "As for expression of affection . . . the stronger the affection, the less inclination have I to express it. Yet sometimes I think myself the most frank, open, and communicative of beings, and at other times the most reserved." [15] How many of us, again, resolve, as she did, when a friend mourned over not having told a lost child how much she loved him, that we will not make the same mistake, but will give our feelings full expression, while there is yet time? The time passes, till it grows too late, and all against our will our lips are sealed.

The depth and the varying phases of Mrs. Stowe's love of her husband are naturally not fully seen in her published letters. That she did love him, both before marriage and after, is evident enough. With the writer's instinct of analysis, she makes a curious dissection of her feelings to a friend, half an hour before her wedding: "Well, my dear, I have been dreading and dreading the time, and lying awake wondering how I should live through this overwhelming crisis, and lo! it has come, and I feel *nothing at all*." [16] But neither the dread nor the indifference indicates any doubt or coldness as to Professor Stowe. When she writes of him to others, it is with a warm efflorescence of praise. His tenderness enwraps her, his enthusiasm upholds her, his confidence sustains her. When she writes to him directly, their mutual understanding and intimate affection are obvious in every line. Amusing stories are told of his occasional assertion of being something more than Mrs. Stowe's husband; but these never imply any jealousy or undue sensitiveness in one who was well qualified to play his part in life without being the husband of anybody.

II

LIKE many writers, and some who have been among the most successful, Mrs. Stowe was neither a great scholar nor a great reader of the writings of others. She speaks of her enjoyment in early childhood of the poetry of Scott. Later, after looking in dismay at the appalling collection of theology in her father's library, she was able to divert herself with the odd agglomeration of fact and fancy in Mather's "Magnalia." As her education went on, she of course became familiar with the standard books which, as names at any rate, are known to intelligent people. She also read curiously such writings of contemporaries as appealed to her quick and eager spirit. But she created her own work from what she saw in life, not from what she found in books. She had neither the vast zest for knowledge as such which is so evident in Margaret Fuller and Sarah Ripley, nor the enthusiasm for education as a moral agent which animated Mary Lyon. Quotations and literary references are not frequent in her letters or in her formal writings. It is the same with artistic matters generally. In later years European travel trained her to a good deal of interest in pictures and architecture. But her temperament was not naturally æsthetic, nor was it especially susceptible to emotional stimulus from painting or music.

The great activity, the really vital and vivid manifestation of her spiritual life, was in religion. When she was twelve years old, she wrote a composition entitled, "Can the Immortality of the Soul be proved by the Light of Nature?" It is a truly appalling production for a child of that age—not in itself, but when one thinks of all it meant in the way of wearing, haunting, morbid spiritual discipline and suggestion.

The young person of to-day cannot realize what these religious problems were to the young person of one hundred years ago. The atmosphere which was breathed from morning to night was loaded with discussion and controversy. Nobody understood this better than Mrs. Stowe, or has depicted it more powerfully. "On some natures," she says, "theology operates as a subtle poison; and the New England theology in particular, with its intense clearness, its sharp-cut crystalline edges and needles of thought, has had in a peculiar degree the power of lacerating the nerves of the soul, and producing strange states of morbid horror and repulsion." [17] Elsewhere she puts this influence even more forcibly: "With many New England women at this particular period, when life was so retired and so cut off from outward sources of excitement, *thinking* grew to be a disease." [18]

If such statements were true in general, even of girls who had the ordinary surroundings of this world and were not especially bound to the atmosphere of the sanctuary, they were far more applicable to Mrs. Stowe herself. Her family was essentially Levitical, and the quintessence of theological excitement was distilled about her dreaming childhood. Her father, Lyman Beecher, was a giant of the faith. He was a robust, active, naturally healthy spirit, a dynamic creature, who used to shovel sand from one corner of the cellar to another to tone his bodily muscles, and toned the muscles of his spirit by shoveling sinners to heaven or to hell. He was born too normal to suffer, himself, the extreme agonies of a tormented conscience, though his curious " Autobiography " shows that even the normal had their struggles to go through.

When it came to a sensitive nervous organization like his daughter's, the spiritual tumult that he spread around him had a far different effect. No doubt she was only one of many; but we have the advantage of a keener insight into her sufferings than into those of others. No doubt there was a certain strange pleasure in the sufferings themselves, an intense, thrilling appreciation of being at any rate alive, such as is quaintly indicated in the brief sentence of Anatole France, "It is sweet to believe, even in hell." Yet, as we read the story of Mrs. Stowe's experiences from our modern point of view, we rebel a little, with the feeling that there is enough unavoidable misery in the world without adding the distresses of the imagination.

What these distresses were in Mrs. Stowe's case we gather from many passages in her letters. That her sensitiveness, her response to influences of joy and depression, to every suggestion from others, was extreme, is everywhere evident. "I believe that there never was a person more dependent on the good and evil opinions of those around than I am." [19] That she took all her spiritual experiences with passion, is evident also. "Thought, intense emotional thought, has been my disease." [20]

The weight of original sin upon such a temperament, the horror of it, with all its fearful consequences, may easily be imagined. An ideal of perfection was before her always, and it seemed as if she never attained it, — and of course she never did. She could do nothing right. Temptations daily beset her and she daily yielded. Back of all her sins was pride, fierce, devilishly prompting pride, the old, stubborn, willful, unconquerable self. She went hourly into battle with it. Sometimes she triumphed for a moment; but it rose again, in hydra variety, forever.

All this was forced in upon her soul, beaten in upon it. You are irretrievably wicked, said her best friends; there is no escape but one: believe — you must believe. So she believed, or said she did, and tried to — tried by day and by night to find her way through the complex maze of doctrine which believing meant in those days. At moments she felt that she had succeeded. Rest came, a wide peace settled down upon her; it seemed that she could never again be troubled any more. "My whole soul was illumined with joy, and as I left the church to walk home, it seemed to me as if Nature herself were hushing her breath to hear the music of heaven." [21] She said to her father, in ecstasy, "Father, I have given myself to Jesus, and He has taken me." And her father answered, as much rejoiced as she, "Then has a new flower blossomed in the kingdom this day."

But the ecstasies did not endure. Do they ever, did they ever, even in the calmest and most saintly heart? Doubts come, difficulties, sometimes a flush of rebellion. She hears preachers say that we have no plea to offer for our sins and no excuse. Have we not? she says. Why were we put into the world with the fierce thirst for sin and so helpless to resist it? "I have never known the time when I have not had a temptation within me so strong that it was certain I should not overcome it." [22]

Worse than the doubts is the dead feeling of exhaustion and emptiness that follows enthusiasm. You are in heaven for an hour. An hour afterwards you do not care whether you are in heaven or in hell. The terrible struggle of these experiences has dried her mind and withered her soul. "Though young, I have no sympathy with the feelings of youth." [23] So her spirit flutters in an endless turmoil, exalted and depressed all the more because of the quiet and tranquillity of her life without.

It is needless to say that she fought through the storm, that with the passage of years she retained the essence of her faith, at the same time dropping or obscuring the struggles and terrors of it. The world was broadening about her and she broadened fully with it. Love came to be the great stronghold of her religion, love and hope and sunshine. She grew more and more willing to leave the mysteries and the problems to take care of themselves.

III

BUT whatever religion she had, it was a primary instinct to preach it. She was not essentially a mystic, content to enjoy her spiritual ecstasies in solitude, to brood over them without any effort to extend them to others. She was born to be active, to be energetic, to make the world feel her existence. When she was a little child, she heard somebody read the Declaration of Independence and it made her "long to do something, I knew not what: to fight for my country, or to make some declaration on my own account." [24] She was like the young college graduate just engaged, who was found in tears and explained that she "wanted to do something for the world and for Wellesley and for him."

In the New England of those days the desire to do
something generally meant to communicate one's religious experiences. This of course involved making
others extremely wretched; but as it was to save their
souls, what did it matter? Had not one been extremely
wretched one's self? So many of these quiet, earnest,
simple women had fought through a passionate spiritual
struggle to a hardly earned and hardly sustained victory! The great impulse of their lives was to fight
the battle and win the victory for those they loved,
for an even wider world, for every one. Each new
battle in a new soul made their own triumphs more
confirmed and sure. If this was the case with women
in general, how much more so was it with one who had
grown up in an atmosphere of preaching and teaching;
whose father had spent his life wrestling with the devil
in the pulpit and in the study and had worsted him glori-
ously; whose brothers had followed the same career
with like energy and success! She speaks of one of these
brothers as *"peppering* the land with moral influence."[25]
Was it not certain that, with her temperament and her
experiences, she would want, in some shape or other, to
hold the pepper-pot herself?

She did. It must not be understood from this that in
daily life she was pedantic, or inclined to moralize and

sermonize. On the contrary, she was gay and sympathetic. She had a wide appreciation of human nature, a wide comprehension of it; and this led her to bear with others whose point of view was entirely different from hers. "Tolerance," she says in one of her books, "tolerance for individual character is about the last Christian grace that comes to flower in family or church." [26] It had come to flower with her. Men and women might differ vastly in beliefs, in standards, even in practice, and yet be all lovable. "My dear friend," she says, "we must consider other people's natures." [27] Is it possible to give more broadly human as well as more broadly Christian advice than that?

But all the tolerance and comprehension did not mean indifference or mere idle study of men's various ways of going to ruin. With the sympathy came a passionate desire to help, a profound conviction that sympathy was the best agent for helping. And as she had a constant eagerness to make over souls, so she had a whirlwind energy in the manner of doing it. She tells us of her father's wonderful faculty of exciting family enthusiasm. When he had an object to accomplish, he would work the whole household up to a pitch of fervent zeal, in which the strength of each one seemed quadrupled. She amply inherited the trait, and strove with all her nervous force to do good, wherever she might be. Even the simple pursuit of her own pleasure she was fain to justify by some side-issue of benevolence. Thus, when she bought a plantation in Florida, she urged that she was largely influenced by the wish to elevate the people. The plan, she says, "is not in any sense a mere worldly enterprise." [28]

Very characteristic is the anecdote told by Elizabeth Stuart Phelps of the friend in Germany whom Mrs. Stowe was anxious to convert from his sceptical philosophy. First, she argued, pleaded, persuaded by letter, some of her letters being even thirty pages long. When this epistolary effort failed her, she was obliged to rely wholly upon prayer; and at length, at Christmas-time, her perseverance was rewarded by the complete conversion of the reluctant German. [29]

But with Mrs. Stowe the natural expression for this preaching, reforming impulse was literature, just as with Mary Lyon it was teaching. Gautier said that the production of copy was a natural function with George Sand. Without emphasizing it quite so strongly, it may yet be said that the pen was the implement that Mrs. Stowe handled most readily and with most pleasure. She did not write because she read. She wrote because she thought and felt, and writing was to her the simplest medium for getting rid of thought and feeling. Like many others with a similar gift, she was not frank or particularly outspoken in daily converse. It costs her an effort to express feeling of any kind, she says. Yet when she took her pen, all her inner life flowed out readily. Could she have said to any one what she wrote of Niagara, for instance? "I felt as if I could have *gone over* with the waters; it would be so beautiful a death; there would be no fear in it. I felt the rock tremble under me with a sort of joy. I was so maddened that I could have gone too, if it had gone." [30]

All her life writing excited her, overpowered her. She does not do it methodically, systematically, but with a frenzy of self-forgetfulness. "*My own book,* instead of cooling, boils and bubbles daily and nightly." [31] The work overcomes her in the production; it overcomes her afterwards, as if it were the production of some one else. When she reads of the death of Uncle Tom, she can "scarcely restrain the convulsion of tears and sobbings" that shakes her frame. [32]

With such a mighty instrument of preaching at hand as this, how can she fail to exercise it? It is a most interesting study to disentangle the web of motives that lies behind her literary achievement. Money? Money enters in, of course. Mrs. Stowe liked to earn. She also liked to spend and liked to give. Now earning was irregular, spending was lamentably regular. She so managed that she was never seriously hampered financially; she was too prudent and too honorable for that. But the pressure of money needs was not strictly favorable to the pursuit of literature. Her biographers tell us that at times what she pursued was not literature, but the necessities of life; and she herself says that when she began "Uncle Tom," she was "driven to write by the necessity of making some income for family expenses." [33]

Yet the passion for writing, for doing something that would make the world remember her, went far deeper than any need of money. Her sister, in a sharp, brief characterization of all the family, says that, as a child, "Harriet is just as odd, and loves to be laughed at as much as ever." [34] To be laughed at, to be pointed at, to be praised — there is the writer surely. Mrs. Stowe tells us that, when she first began to read, she was possessed with the longing to do something in literature. When she was thirteen, she wrote a tragedy. "It filled my thoughts sleeping and waking," [35] till her sister forced her to write extracts from Butler's "Analogy," instead. All through the production of her lengthy series of works it is evident that she was impelled by something besides the need of money: that the intense ambition to succeed, to get glory, to touch and move and thrill the hearts of men, was ever present with her.

At the same time, she would not have admitted that this was her main motive, any more than money. Her gifts, if she had any, were given her for a purpose, and that was never forgotten. "He has given me talents and I will lay them at his feet, well satisfied if He will accept them." [36] She writes with her life-blood, she says, and "as called of God." In "Uncle Tom" she was openly and confessedly doing missionary work. But in everything she ever wrote, her desire was the same. She was a Beecher. The Beechers were Levites, preachers, all of them, — only it fell to her to hold forth from a vaster pulpit than any other Beecher ever dreamed of. And just as with them, so her utterances were given to her from a higher source. She did not write "Uncle Tom," she declares. She saw it, she felt it, she heard it in prophetic visions. It came to her in a great tide of inspiration, the spirit pouring through her as its mere humble instrument for the renovation and regeneration of the world.

And as the preaching, missionary instinct was always present in her literary ambition, so it was equally present in her enjoyment of popularity and success. It is unnecessary to say that these came to her in vast measure, and she appreciated them. When she was eleven years old, her father asked her teacher who wrote a certain composition. "Your daughter, sir."[37] "It was the proudest moment of my life," she says. But she had many proud moments afterwards. The storm of applause — and of equally intoxicating obloquy — which came to her from "Uncle Tom's Cabin" has not often been surpassed in the history of literature. She was praised and admired and reviled in America. In England the reviling was less, the praise and admiration perhaps even greater. When she visited that country, high and low crowded to gaze upon her, to touch her hand, to hear her speak.

Nor was it all vague and impersonal glory which flowed about her in the streets but left her alone on an isolated pinnacle. What she asked of the world most was love. In the full sweep of her success she wrote, "It is not fame nor praise that contents me. I seem never to have needed love so much as now."[38] Well, love came to her. She made friends everywhere, friends with wealth, friends with distinction, friends with titles, who took her into their hearts just as nearly as those who had grown up with her at home. The warm lining of her fame was as rich and lasting as its glittering outside.

Through it all she was modest, put on no airs or vain

pretenses, did not seem to feel that she had done anything great, insisted, with apparent sincerity, that the
work was not her work, nor hers the glory. She moved
among those curious and applauding crowds, a little,
quiet, shrinking yet always dignified figure, with a half
smile of wonder what they were all making such a fuss
about. "It was enough to frighten a body into fits," says
her husband of one great occasion. " But we took it as
quietly as we could, and your mamma looked as meek
as Moses in her little, battered straw hat and gray cloak,
seeming to say, 'I didn't come here o' purpose.'" [39]

She enjoyed it; oh, there is no doubt about that. She
was eminently human, and few human beings have lived
who would not have enjoyed it. But through all the
tumult and hurly-burly there persisted that still, small
voice telling her that the triumph and the means that
won it were given her for a purpose. The instinct of
the missionary and preacher at once excused her joy in
her success and doubled it. Not hers was it to write
brilliant and cleverly turned stories for the fleeting en-
chantment of an hour, but to stir hearts, to win hearts,
to push on the movement of great causes in a turbid
world.

Lowell, writing as editor of the "Atlantic," of which
she was a pillar in those days, cautioned her to "Let

your moral take care of itself, and remember that an author's writing-desk is something infinitely higher than a pulpit." [40]

(To her there was nothing higher than a pulpit, nothing could be.) "The power of fictitious writing, for good as well as evil, is a thing which ought most seriously to be reflected on," [41] she says. She never ceased to reflect on it.

IV

SHE reflected on it more than she did on her story, her incidents, or her characters. In fact, fortunately, these hurried her on without reflection. But plenty of the reflection on the power of fictitious writing for good and evil always got mixed up with them. By temperament she was an interested and an acute and exact observer of human nature, both external and internal. Her stories, all her stories in greater or less degree, are founded on an extensive study of character and manners. This is true of her Southern novels, and they show that she had made good use of her opportunities in collecting material, both consciously and unconsciously. It is far more true of her New England books; and the fine and varied insight of "The Minister's Wooing," "The Pearl of Orr's Island," especially of "Oldtown Folks," has hardly been surpassed since. In this line it must be remembered that Mrs. Stowe was an originator, for Hawthorne's work was entirely different in spirit. If Miss Jewett, Mrs. Freeman, and Miss Alice Brown have developed some sides more effectively, Mrs. Stowe deserves credit for having set the great example. The shrewdness, the sympathy, with which she depicted the New England farmer, and, above all, his wife and daughter, are forever commendable and delightful. That peculiar thing called the New England conscience is especially fascinating to Mrs. Stowe, and she is never weary of disentangling its curious webs of subtle torment.

In making all these investigations she sometimes likes to think of herself as the artist merely, who portrays man's body and soul with scientific ardor and is more concerned with truth than with moral efficacy. "I am myself but the observer and reporter," she writes, "seeing much, doubting much, questioning much, and believing with all my heart only in a very few things."[42] She does herself infinite injustice. By comparison with some of us, she believed in a great many things. Especially, she was filled with an overwhelming zeal to convey to others what beliefs she had. It is here that she differs from the notable writers who have succeeded her. They, for the most part, observe and report life as it is, from scientific and artistic curiosity. But to Mrs. Stowe every heart is a text and every tragedy a fearful example. She probably was not aware herself how furiously she preached. But no Beecher was ever a mere observer, or could have been contented to leave New England and the world without making them better.

And as her observation and material were affected by her missionary spirit, so her artistic methods were affected even more. Everywhere the illustration of human truth is a secondary object; the first is to produce an effect — naturally, a moral effect. Now, in literature the subordination of truth to effect, no matter for what purpose, is melodrama. Dumas and the thousands like him arrange effective incident merely to amuse, to startle and excite the reader; Mrs. Stowe arranges it to jolt the reader into the path of virtue. It is not a question of violent sensation. Where are there more violent sensations than are to be found in Shakespeare? But, as Trollope admirably remarks, there is no objection to sensation, no matter how violent, provided it is always subordinated to the development of character. When character is subordinated to sensation, the proper name is surely melodrama. It is amusing and profitable to hear Mrs. Stowe herself on this subject. Some one has accused her of being moved by melodrama. She is at first appalled, though she has no very clear idea what is meant. Then she concludes consolingly, "If, by being melodramatic, as the terrible word is, he [the painter] can shadow forth a grand and comforting religious idea . . . who shall say that he may not do so because he violates the lines of some old Greek artist?"[43] You see the point.

An entertaining side-issue of this preaching aspect of the creator of Uncle Tom is her active part in the Byron controversy. I have no wish to stir up a vexed and disagreeable question; but I do insist that Mrs. Stowe's part in it was based upon the zealous desire to do good, however much lack of tact she may have shown. When she was a child, she adored Byron, and was deeply overcome by the announcement of his death. She heard it from her father, who also adored him, — with reservations, — and thought that, if Byron "could only have talked with Taylor and me, it might have got him out of his troubles."[44] Isn't that delicious? Later, she became intimate with Lady Byron, and, after her death, felt that an effort to make clear her relations with her husband was a necessary act of justice to the memory of a long maligned woman. And what a magnificent theme it was for moral edification! Still, you see, the preacher Beecher. For it cannot be denied that there hung always about Mrs. Stowe that light, vast aura of sanctification which is, or was, so apt to emanate from the New England ministerial being, and which is condensed into a supernatural glow upon the countenance, even pictured, of her distinguished brother, Henry Ward.

I do not mean, however, to stress this missionary side of Mrs. Stowe with undue emphasis. As I have before pointed out, she was a sunny, human person, with large understanding of the weaknesses of others and large allowance for them. She had an excellent portion of humor in her composition, and indeed this was as characteristic of her family as was preaching. She says of her oldest sister that her "life seemed to be a constant stream of mirthfulness;"[45] and Harriet herself often drifted into broad eddies of the same golden river. From her father she inherited the faculty of amusing people as well as that of admonishing them. From him also she got a sense of the pleasant things of this world, and a sort of eternal youth for enjoying them. "Hearts never grow old, do they?" cried the Reverend Lyman; and his daughter could have said the same.

One even divines in Mrs. Stowe pagan possibilities

that are really delightful. She reproaches George Eliot with too much self-abnegation, and wishes that she could get her into the Beecher household, where "we sometimes make the rafters ring with fun, and say anything and everything, no matter what." [46] She has occasionally an obscure feeling that something is wrong in the preaching attitude; that there are interests in life besides being good and the effect to make others so. "With all New England's earnestness and practical efficiency," she writes, "there is a long withering of the soul's more ethereal part, — a crushing out of the beautiful, — which is horrible. Children are born there with a sense of beauty equally delicate with any in the world, in whom it dies a lingering death of smothered desire and pining, weary starvation. I know, because I have felt it." [47]

What charms me most in this connection is Mrs. Stowe's conversion to Rubens. In all the wide spiritual world can you imagine temperaments more different? She knew it as well as you do. She begins by hating him. Yet even then she feels the power. "Rubens, whose pictures I detested with all the energy of my soul, I knew and felt all the time, by the very pain he gave me, to be a real living artist." [48] Afterwards, when she sees the gorgeous Medici group in Paris, she is almost, if not quite, converted. That starved childish spirit which hungered for earthly loveliness in the barren New England desert found something to thrill it in the Rubens flesh, so splendidly redolent of the glory of this world. In fact, if she had been a pagan suckled in a creed outworn, she would have followed it with the same proselyting ardor that she gave to Christianity; and the image of Mrs. Stowe, a thyrsus in her hand, undraped in a dainty, if limited, garment of fawnskin, careering over the pastures by the sea, at the head of a Bacchic squadron of middle-aged New England matrons, does not lack a certain piquant, if indecorous, exhilaration.

But she was to descend to posterity, not as a votaress of Bacchus, but as an ardent expositor of the New England conscience. All her books are saturated with it. In every one of them nature and human nature, passion and hope, good and ill, are used to illustrate the goodness of God, the importance of virtue, the absolute necessity of making over the world on the New England model. Perhaps "Uncle Tom's Cabin" is no better than some of the others; but it has the characteristics of all of them, and a fortunate conjunction of circumstances gave it an enormous success which none of the others could have achieved. Read everywhere in America and Europe, translated into all languages, a mighty instrument in the extinction of slavery, it was far more than a novel, it was one of the greatest moral agencies the world has seen; and Mrs. Stowe will be simply the author of it to millions who know, and care to know, nothing else about her. Few teachers or preachers anywhere can ever hope to accomplish such results as she did.

Undeniably, with Mrs. Stowe, as with others of her type, there are times when one wearies intensely of this missionary endeavor. After all, the sky is blue, the winds blow, and life is pleasant. Why not let it go at that? Yet, when the hours and days of anguish come, — for the individual or for the world, — as they are coming now, we realize that perhaps we need these little, fragile, insinuating, indomitable things with curls to drive or wheedle us into the fold of God.

V
MARGARET FULLER OSSOLI

CHRONOLOGY

Sarah Margaret Fuller
Born in Cambridge, Massachusetts, May 23, 1810.
Grew up in Cambridge and Groton.
Taught and talked in Boston and elsewhere, 1837–1844.
Edited the "Dial," 1840–1842.
Literary Life in New York, 1844–1846.
In Europe, 1846–1850.
Married the Marquis Ossoli, December, 1847.
Drowned off Fire Island, July 19, 1850.

MARGARET FULLER OSSOLI

MARGARET FULLER OSSOLI

I

SARAH MARGARET FULLER brought the thrill of life wherever she went, though she was often only half alive herself. As a child, from 1820 to 1830, she stirred her Cambridge playmates. As a teacher and talker she stirred the transcendental circles of Boston. As a writer in New York she moved men and women with her soul more than with her pen. She went to Italy in the forties and the Italians loved her, and one of them made her a marchioness and a mother. Then the stormy sea engulfed her, as it did Shelley.

Mrs. Cheney, writing in 1902, fifty years after Margaret's death, says: " She is the woman of America who is moulding the lives and the characters of her country-women more than any other. It is for her that in the new West, which she was among the first to understand, the women's clubs are named, and both in the East and West audiences gladly listen to all that can be told of her."[1] I wonder if this is as true to-day as it was then.

The best way to understand Margaret will be to analyze her in three distinct phases, to unfold, as it were, one wrapping after another, until we reach the essential secret of her heart. And first we should see her in that social contact with others which, at any rate in the earlier part of her life, was her ambition and her despair. No one has striven harder than she to accomplish in human relations what those who strive hardest recognize most clearly in the end to be impossible.

As a woman, if we are to consider her socially, we must begin by thinking of her appearance. She had a passionate longing to be beautiful; but apparently no one thought her so. She was rather short, rather heavy, had a lofty but not attractive carriage, opened and shut her eyes oddly, poised her head oddly. Emerson says that she "made a disagreeable first impression on most persons . . . to such an extreme that they did not wish to be in the same room with her."[2] She grew aware of this with time, though perhaps she did not wholly understand the causes. I "made up my mind," she says, "to be bright and ugly."[3]

She was bright enough, but there was too much making up the mind about it, and it did not please strangers, —nor even, in the early days, people who knew her well. A tradition of intense dislike still surrounds her name for many who can never get over it. Horace Mann, suggesting a popular impression about her family, said that "she had the disagreeableness of forty Fullers,"[4] and certainly at times she did appear to concentrate a large dose of the unattractive. "To the multitude she was a haughty and supercilious person,"[5] says one who admired and loved her. However much she may have prized attention and applause, she would not stoop for them. It is doubtful whether the records of history show a woman who began life by declaring, to herself and others, a larger and more sweeping sense of her own power and importance. Her mighty and four-square egotism teased the shy and self-distrustful Hawthorne till he had immortalized it in the Zenobia of the "Blithedale Romance." It disconcerted the grave Emerson. It annoyed Lowell, — "A very foolish, conceited woman."[6] It amused Horace Greeley, who was not without his own fair share of the same quality. The pleasant interplay of the two egotisms together is delightfully illustrated in Margaret's comment on Horace: "His abilities, in his own way, are great. He believes in mine to a surprising extent. We are true friends."[7] But nothing can equal Margaret's own words about herself. "There are also in every age a few in whose lot the meaning of that age is concentrated. I feel that I am one of those persons in my age and sex. I feel chosen among women."[8] And again, "I now know all the people worth knowing in America, and I find no intellect comparable to my own."[9] She was fully developed and mature when she said this, and I do not know where you can surpass it. With all her brilliancy and all her wit, perhaps she lacked the sense of humor that might have saved her from the worst excesses of egotism.

To be sure, more think these things than say them, and we must accredit Margaret with a royal candor which is not without charm. She said what she thought about herself, and she said what she thought about others right to their faces. Those who were large enough came to appreciate the spirit in which she did it. But many were not large enough, and her best friends admit that she combined candor with a singular and unfortunate tactlessness.

It must not be supposed, however, that Margaret nursed, or wished to nurse, her self-esteem in private. I have said that she sought society. She did, and with the wish to dominate and control it, to be the leader, if anything at all. In this respect, as in some others, she recalls Lady Holland, who for so many years maintained a salon by sheer force of will. Margaret "had an immense appetite for social intercourse,"[10] says one who knew her intimately, and she threw herself into this, as into everything, with the furious ardor which she herself understood so well. "There is no modesty or moderation in me."[11] Wherever she came, she wished to lead, and to dominate whomsoever she met. Yield to her, and she would love you — if she thought you worth while. Resist her, and you became an object of interest, whether she thought you worth while or not. Emerson says: "When a person was overwhelmed by her, and answered not a word except 'Margaret, be merciful to me, a sinner,' then her love and tenderness would come like a seraph's."[12]

The means she used to ensnare and captivate were as varied as they were startling. She would adapt herself to every one, be all things to all men and women, if the fancy seized her. Persuasion was just as much at her command as force. Her powers of imitation and mimicry were unlimited. "Had she condescended to appear before the footlights, she would soon have been recognized as the first actress of the Nineteenth Century,"[13] says Greeley. We have often heard before of ladies who would have been, if they had condescended. Nevertheless, the tribute is important for the study of Margaret. Read, also, her own autobiographical story, "Mariana," with its extraordinary account of her attempts as a child at boarding-school to control and dominate her fellow pupils, the arts and wiles and deceptions she cunningly practiced only to overthrow her influence in the end by her impatient haughtiness and eccentricity. She had, she says of herself, "the same power of excitement that is described in the spinning dervishes of the East. Like them she would spin until all around her were giddy, while her own brain, instead of being disturbed, was excited to great action." [14] Read, also, Emerson's description of the means she used to overcome his original prejudice: "She studied my tastes, piqued and amused me, challenged frankness by frankness, and did not conceal the good opinion of me she brought with her, nor her wish to please. She was curious to know my opinions and experiences. Of course, it was impossible long to hold out against such urgent assault." [15]

So others found it besides Emerson. For it must be recognized that this singular creature, who had such a power of making enemies and arousing distaste, had also such immense mental and spiritual resources that her talk was admired and her society sought by the wisest and the wittiest persons who came near her. To begin with, she had a belief in conversation, its delights and possibilities, which seems pathetic to those who have pursued the ideal of it through an Odyssey of failure. She loved to talk, to make others talk, even to try to make others talk. It must be confessed that, by universal testimony, she had an extraordinary power of stimulation, of taking what seemed to be dull clods and making hearts of them. Madame Arconati wrote Emerson that she had known no woman with a mind *plus vivifiant*.[16] The word seems final. Her soul touched others and made them live.

All records of these wonderful talkers, all attempts to transmit them to posterity, are more or less unsuccessful. But Margaret has been fortunate in her interpreters. They rarely note her words, but, wisely, the impression she made upon them. And it is easy to gather what her power of adaptation was in different surroundings. For instance, Horace Greeley found her serious, in the main. "She *could* be joyous and even merry; but her usual manner, while with us, was one of grave thoughtfulness, absorption in noble deeds, and in paramount aspirations."[17] How different is Emerson's picture! He does not, indeed, deny the gravity. She could and would talk with ravishing earnestness, and with a frankness, as from man to man, which no man could excel. But what sudden and surprising changes from gravity to mirth, what echoing gayety, what swift and stinging satire, what instant gift of adjustment to the call of circumstance! "She sympathizes so fast with all forms of life, that she talks never narrowly or hostilely, nor betrays, like all the rest, under a thin garb of new words, the old droning cast-iron opinions or notions of many years' standing." [18] And the same excellent judge sums up her talk as "the most entertaining conversation in America." [19] Again, he says of her power over those she met: "Of personal influence, speaking strictly, — an efflux, that is, purely of mind and character, excluding all effects of power, wealth, fashion, beauty, or literary fame — she had an extraordinary degree; I think more than any person I have known." [20] That this could be said of one who had the exceptional elements of repulsion noted in the beginning of this portrait shows that we are dealing with a soul of unusual and fascinating interest.

Nor was Margaret's power over the hearts of others merely an external, temporary, and social one. She could not only startle and stimulate; where she chose, she could inspire profound and lasting attachment. "I at least," says Colonel Higginson, "have never known any woman who left behind an affection so deep and strong. It is now thirty years since her death, and there is scarcely a friend of hers who does not speak of her with as warm a devotion as if she had died yesterday." [21]   During a part of her life Margaret was a teacher. She taught in various schools and in different places. Under her teaching should also be included her curious attempt to combine the methods of Greek academies and French salons in the public assemblies, held in Boston, which she called conversations. It would be easy to cite abundant ridicule of these latter performances. Miss Martineau and many others found them terribly pedantic, and the element of pedantry was not lacking in them. Yet it is incontestable that those who came most under Margaret's influence, either in this way or in her more formal teaching, found an inspiration that lasted them for life. Her own comment on her gifts hits us like a cold-water douche: "My great talent at explanation, tact in the use of means, and immediate and invariable power over the minds of my pupils." [22]   But when one of the pupils says the same thing, we cannot but accept it: "I had no idea that I should esteem and, much more, love her. I found myself in a new world of thought; a flood of light irradiated all that I had seen in nature, observed in life, or read in books." [23]

'And all this adoration was not dumb, remote, or incapable of personal transference. What strikes one most of all in Margaret's relation to her fellows is her unusual faculty of eliciting confession from the most varying sources. One does not commonly expect this in persons of such pronounced and self-assertive temperament. But it cannot be denied in her. Emerson was immensely impressed by it: "She drew her companions to surprising confessions."[24] Another observer, who had himself a similar experience, regards it as phenomenal: "I judge that she was the repository of more confidences than any contemporary," he says. "Women who had known her but a day revealed to her the most jealously guarded secrets of their lives. . . . Nor were these revelations made only by those of her own plane of life, but chambermaids and seamstresses unburdened their souls to her, seeking and receiving her counsel; while children found her a delightful playmate and a capital friend."[25]

Various elements enter into the explanation of this gift of Margaret's of drawing out others' souls. As to one of these elements all observers unite: she never betrayed a confidence that had been placed in her. But there was far more to it than that, — she entered into the lives and hearts of others with the widest imaginative comprehension. She does, indeed, in a moment of discouragement, deny herself sympathy: "a person all intellect and passion, no loveliness of character; impetuous, without tender sympathy."[26] But even as to emotional sympathy she belied herself. And her power of understanding souls of all colors and complexions, of entering into quick passion and aspiration as well as slow despair, was almost unlimited. Under the surface that seemed dull and dead to others she saw the glowing spark and her breath kindled it into vital fire. She made lives over. Especially she was "the interpreter and savior of women," says Mrs. Cheney, "for there was no questioning, no suffering, that had not passed through the alembic of her imagination and thought, if not of her actual experience. . . . The largeness of her life and thoughts made her a great helper."[27]

II

WITH this largeness of life and thought we may pass from Margaret's social and external relations with others to the inner activity of her intelligence. It may be said at once that hers was not above all a logically creative mind. She thought out no speculative systems, nor even gave herself with slow industry to criticizing the systems of others. But her intellect was keen, vivid, illuminating,—dashed right into the heart of a subject or of a person, plucked out the essential nucleus for herself and others to behold, and then passed on. She hated prejudice and convention, wanted the primal elements of things, even things distressing and hateful. "With her," she said of a friend, "I can talk of anything. She is like me. She is able to look facts in the face." [28] And again, with bitter ardor: "In the chamber of death, I prayed in very early years, 'Give me truth; cheat me by no illusion.'" [29] She had a splendid analytical power, which shows more in brief touches from casual writings than in her formal works. Thus, of a conversation with Emerson: "He is a much better companion than formerly, — for once he would talk obstinately through the walk, but now we can be silent and see things together." [30] Or more generally: "We need to hear the excuses men make to themselves for their worthlessness." [31]

As is natural and unavoidable, with a person who has this gift of analysis, she applied it first of all and constantly to herself. True, she felt that she accomplished little and got nowhere, and this recognition is the surest mark of her power. "I know little about the mystery of life, and far less in myself than in others." [32] Yet she probed and probed, with inexhaustible, quiet, curious diligence, and she is not one of the least profitable of the anatomizers of soul. Hear her on the near approach of death. "On this subject I always feel that I can speak with some certainty, having been on the verge of bodily dissolution. I felt at that time disengaged from the body, hovering, and calm." [33] Again and again she speaks of herself with quiet detachment, judging her own character and conduct, good and evil, exactly as if she were appraising somebody else. One who had long known her family says that they were peculiar in speaking out openly all the things which we commonly suppress about ourselves and express only about other people. This was certainly true of Margaret. For instance, when she writes to her brother, urging him to make sacrifices for the younger children, she points out all that she had given up for him. "I do not say this to pain you, or to make you more grateful to me (for, probably, if I had been aware at the time what I was doing, I might not have sacrificed myself so)." [34]

As I have suggested earlier, it is to this exceptional instinct of analysis and calm-eyed candor that we are to attribute largely those violent expressions of egotism which are so astonishing. When Margaret sighs, "Oh that my friends would teach me that 'simple art of not too much!' How can I expect them to bear the ceaseless eloquence of my nature?"[35] she is really sighing and not posing at all. Indeed, with the perfectly candid recognition of her powers, she combined often a yearning humility, a deep desire to correct herself of many faults. How charming is the comment, in her earlier love letters, on a friend who was inclined to criticize her weaknesses — or excess of strength: "I think, too, with one whose judgment I valued, I should receive fault-finding in the spirit in which it was meant, and if it gave me pain, should be more likely to mend than many who take it more easily."[36] While perhaps something even nobler and larger than humility permeates the royal sentence, so often quoted but not too often, "I feel as if there was plenty of room in the universe for my faults, and as if I could not spend time in thinking of them, when so many things interest me more."[37]

It is in connection with the profound study of her own nature as well as of the nature of others that we should consider her interesting and elaborate theories of self-development, self-culture, constant spiritual progress. In this she was no doubt greatly influenced by Goethe, who was more of a force in her mental life than any other figure of the past. It is easy to make fun of such deliberate preoccupation with one's self, and most of us will maintain that action rather than reflection is the true means of self-development. The greater part of Hawthorne's savage and absurdly exaggerated attack on Margaret is based upon a ludicrous over-estimate of her attempts to revolutionize herself. "It was such an awful joke, that she should have re-solved — in all sincerity, no doubt — to make herself the greatest, wisest, best woman of the age. And to that end she set to work on her strong, heavy, unpliable, and, in many respects, defective and evil nature, and adorned it with a mosaic of admirable qualities, such as she chose to possess; putting in here a splendid talent and there a moral excellence, and polishing each sepa-rate piece, and the whole together, till it seemed to shine afar and dazzle all who saw it. She took credit to her-self for having been her own Redeemer, if not her own Creator." [38]

No one who has carefully studied Margaret's own letters or other writings, or the testimony of those who knew her best, will for a moment accept seriously either these or any other of Hawthorne's severe strictures for more than an outburst of ill-temper. No two char-acters could have been more different than Hawthorne's and Margaret's, or, if they had some points of resem-blance, they would have clashed on those resemblances more than on their differences. As to the self-culture,

too elaborate theories in this line have again and again
defeated themselves in their most intelligent and conscientious exponents. Margaret came to see this in the
end. Yet it cannot be denied that no effort was ever
more conscientious than hers. Nor can it be denied
that the effort was intelligently controlled and that it
effected probably as much as has ever been effected by
any human being. The constitutional disagreeableness
which I have suggested in beginning this study diminished constantly with the progress of years. The nar-
rowness of egotism, largely fostered in youth by seclu-
sion and excessive reading, yielded more and more to
the mellowing influences of wider contact with humanity. In her own noble phrase, she "unlearned contempt";[39] and what positive learning can be finer or
more difficult than that? While both positive and negative advancement are summed up in the earnest motto
which she adopted in her youth and clung to always,
however differently she may have come to interpret it:
"Very early I knew that the only object in life was to
grow."[40]

It is hardly necessary to say that Margaret's theories
of culture included much more than mere book-learning.
Yet her achievements in this line were remarkable. Or
perhaps I should say that her powers were even more

remarkable than her achievements. She herself, in a moment of unusual discouragement, declares: "I have long thought my mind must be as shallow as it is vapid." [41] But it was certainly neither vapid nor shallow. A good judge, who knew her well, speaks of "the rapidity with which she appropriates all knowledge, joined with habits of severe mental discipline (so rare in women, and in literary men not technically 'men of science')." [42] She could grasp the meaning of a book swiftly, fit it to its place in the great scheme of thought and spiritual movement, then hasten to something else, perhaps quite different, and accomplish the same result with equal ease and equal sureness.

Her actual possession of learning was far less than Mrs. Ripley's. She had a less broad and exact command of languages; she took little interest in science, and even in philosophy she could not be called an exhaustive student. To her, — and more and more as she grew older, — books were but the interpreters of life, and her keenest and most thoughtful study was given to the hearts of men.

But the most interesting thing about her studies, as about all her pursuits, is the passion with which she threw herself into them. Her intellectual effort was not a calm and steady flame, like Mrs. Ripley's, burning unaltered and unshaken through all sorts of disturbance and difficulty. She could not turn quietly and serenely from astronomy to botany, from German to mathematics, as convenience suggested and opportunity offered. There were moments of spiritual exaltation and enthusiasm. "I am living like an angel, and I don't know how to get down."[43] But these times were paid for in exhaustion and depression and disgust. "I never can do well more than one thing at a time, and the least thing costs me so much thought and feeling; others have no idea of it."[44] Above all, she lived in perpetual distraction. A thousand cares were ever crowding upon her, and when it was not external cares, it was spiritual vexations and questions and perplexities. "I have learned much and thought little," she complains, "an assertion which seems paradoxical and *is* true. I faint with desire to think . . . but some outward requisition is ever knocking at the door of my mind and I am as ill placed as regards a chance to think as a haberdasher's prentice or the President of Harvard University."[45] So she struggled onward in a constant turmoil of effort and aspiration, and if her mental kingdom was in some respects ill-coördinated and ill-regulated, at least she was always mentally alive.

Alive, too, in other aspects of spiritual sensibility,

besides the merely intellectual. In painting and music, as in thought, what strikes one is rather the effort and passion of her appreciation than its amplitude and security. She touched the great artists widely and sought and fought to make their achievement part of her soul, but she never seems to have entered quite fully into their calm perfection. The same is true of religion. It is interesting and often pathetic to see her humble, earnest desire for the passion of the mystic and the Christian hope. "My mind often burns with thoughts on these subjects and I long to pour out my soul to some person of superior calmness and strength and fortunate in more accurate knowledge. I should feel such a quieting reaction. But generally I think it is best I should go through these conflicts alone."[46] She went through many of them and they resulted in the formulation of the curious "Credo," — not printed until very recently, — which aims at an exactness of definition such as neither Emerson nor Goethe would ever have attempted. Doctrinally it has little interest. As throwing psychological light on Margaret it has much, for example in the splendid and characteristic phrase: "For myself, I believe in Christ because I can do without him."[47]

But the charm of Margaret's sensibility and depth of spiritual emotion shows much better in simpler things than in these more pretentious regions of art and thought. She felt the natural world with peculiar solemnity and intensity. This is evident in her own curious account of the experience of being lost alone for a whole night amid the Highland mountains. It is much more evident in briefer references to New England woods and flowers and fields. You could not find a better antidote to Hawthorne's harsh judgment than this delicate picture of open-air life: "Many, many sweet little things would I tell you, only they are so very little. I feel just now as if I could live and die here. I am out in the open air all the time except about two hours in the early morning. And now the moon is fairly gone late in the evening. While she was here, we staid out, too. Everything seems sweet here, so homely, so kindly; the old people chatting so contentedly, the young men and girls laughing together in the fields — not vulgarly, but in the true kinsfolk way, — little children singing in the house and beneath the berry-bushes." [48] Or take another in which the sense of natural beauty rises into passion: "One night when I was out bathing at the foot of the tall rock, the waters rippling up so gently, the ships gliding full-sailed and dreamy-white over a silver sea, the crags above me with their dewy garlands and the little path stealing away in shadow, oh, it was almost too beautiful to bear and live." [49]

When one reads these things, one wonders why Margaret did not leave a greater name in actual literature, why her very numerous writings are not more read to-day. This is partly owing, no doubt, to the ephemeral nature of her subjects, — travel pictures, controversial essays, criticisms of authors who have not lived themselves. Even in these buried articles there is much shrewd observation that deserves better than to be forgotten. Still, it must be admitted that her formal, printed works do not do her justice. She was better than any of them, and she knew it. She would have liked literary glory and success, none more so. But she had a proud assurance that there was something finer in her than had ever come out. She would not, indeed, have used of herself, nor would we quite have her use, her own words as to a minor writer: "What he does is bad, but full of a great desire." [50] But she does say, as pathetically as justly: "I feel within myself an immense power, but I cannot bring it out." [51] And even better is the noble prophecy which we still believe that the future will maintain: "My health is frail; my earthly life is shrunk to a scanty rill; I am little better than an aspiration, which the ages will reward, by empowering me to incessant acts of vigorous beauty."[52] It was as such an inspiration that she established her conspicuous place among the writers for the "Dial" and the group of transcendentalists who made New England famous in the middle of the nineteenth century.

III

WE have yet to uncover Margaret's heart, to pass deeper from her social and worldly aspect and her intellectual and literary interests to the passion and the struggle of the woman.

To begin with, she was a lover, always a lover, even from her childhood. In her own family, her father, stern like herself with Puritan self-restraint, though he was proud of her and taught her and developed her, did not give her all the tenderness she needed. How much she needed it appears in the passionate words she wrote long after his death: "I recollect how deep the anguish, how deeper still the want, with which I walked alone in hours of childish passion and called for a Father, after saying the word a hundred times."[53] The same depth of tenderness she gave in full measure to her brothers and sisters.

And the tenderness was not mere sentiment but

showed in practical action. Mr. Fuller's death left his family much cramped financially, and Margaret was forced to deny herself, and did deny herself without hesitation, the spiritual opportunities she so much craved that her brothers and sisters might have proper education and advantages. "Let me now try to forget myself and act for others' sakes,"[54] she wrote, and she acted as she wrote. She taught the younger children; she did the mending and the cooking; she took care of her mother, who was often ill, and of her grandmother, who was so always.

She was not only a zealous manager, but a prudent and intelligent one. She understood extremely well the value of money, knew how to husband it, and how to spend it so as to make it go farthest and buy most. She supplied her brothers with caution, yet with wide liberality, considering her limitations. Above all, she stinted herself that she might give, not only in her family but far without. "Her charities, according to her means, were larger than those of any other whom I ever knew,"[55] writes one who had much experience of Margaret—and of others. Even the bitter words wrung from her in the anguish of the last miserable years show only what her generosity had been and what we are sure it was still. "My love for others had turned against me. I had given to other sufferers what I now needed for myself so deeply, so terribly; I shall never again be perfectly, be religiously generous; I understand why others are not. I am worse than I was." [56]

And her human tenderness extended far beyond her own family. We have seen that she wanted to be admired and praised and worshiped. She wanted to be loved, also, and perhaps this was really at the root of the less commendable instinct. Amidst all the popularity and social compliment she keenly appreciated what affection was, — just common affection. "Around my path how much humble love has flowed. These everyday friends never forget my heart, never censure me, make no demands on me, load me with gifts and services, and, uncomplaining, see me prefer my intellectual kindred." [57] She wanted to give love, too, as well as get it. She knew well at all times of her life that aching emptiness which only an overpowering devotion can fill. Do we not get a glimpse of it in the quiet words describing one contact with youth and beauty? "She was a lovely child then, and happy, but my heart ached, and I lived in just the way I do now." [58]

Nothing throws more light on this human craving than Margaret's relation with the good Emerson. They sought and admired each other and got and gave much. But Emerson, who so abounded in kindness, was perhaps somewhat limited in the blind longings of the heart. He speaks of "the romantic sacrifice and ecstatic fusion" [59] of Margaret's friendships, with a humorous acceptance of incomprehension. Margaret herself complains of his coldness, of his incapacity for the highest surrender. "He met men, not as a brother, but as a critic." [60] And it would be amusing, if it were not pathetic, to see her dissatisfaction reflected in Emerson's account of it. She called his friendship commercial, he says, felt that he could not prize affection unless it chattered, weighed love by what he got from it only. He quotes her very words: "The deepest love that approached you was, in your eyes, nothing but a magic lantern, always bringing out pretty shows of life." [61] Some of us to-day feel too keenly what Margaret meant. But, all the same, how noble and beautiful is the humility of Emerson's comment: "As I did not understand the discontent then, — of course, I cannot now." [62]

The question naturally arises, how about love with Margaret in the ordinary sense, how about her relations with men who were not simply friends and philosophers? In her earlier years there is no definite trace of anything of the sort. She had few of the attractions which

draw young men and none of the coquetry which seeks
to draw them. Her youthful letters and reminiscences
do not indicate any affection, requited or unrequited.
Then, in 1844, when she was well over thirty, she fell
in with a brilliant member of the Jewish race, and for
a year she kept up a correspondence with him, which
has been printed by Mrs. Howe, and which shows Margaret as deeply and sentimentally in love as any schoolgirl.

It is true that the old egotism still hangs about her.
Her dear companion is the first she "ever had who could
feel every little shade of life and beauty as exquisitely
as myself." [63] But she relishes even the shock to egotism which comes with the self-abandonment of this
new tenderness. She finds a strange thrill of pleasure
in the lover's admonition, "You must be a fool, little
girl." [64] She indulges in all the fantastic freaks of
amorous imagination, the ardor for an impossible union,
the frantic questionings, the idle self-tormentings, — not
one of the old, well-known symptoms is missing. And
to complete all, she assumes, as usual, that they are first
known to her. As the gay French comedy puts it, *En
voilà encore une qui croit avoir inventé l'amour.*

Yet even these love-letters, earnest as they are, genuine as they are, and most important in the light they

throw upon Margaret's character, are not wholly free from a suggestion of literature. When the infatuation is over, her characteristic comment is: "I shall write a sketch of it and turn the whole to account in a literary way, since the affections and ideal hopes are so unproductive." [65] There had been more head than heart in the matter, and to touch the deepest secrets of her nature required a different temperament from that of the brilliant Jew. After a few months' sojourn in Italy, she found such a temperament, certainly very different, in the Marquis Ossoli, whom she married secretly at the close of the year 1847. Judgments about Ossoli are somewhat varying. The utter brutality of a comment recorded by Hawthorne defeats itself and suggests some obscure ground of prejudice. According to this view the marquis had no claim even to good-breeding, let alone intelligence, "in short, half an idiot, and without any pretension to be a gentleman," [66] and Margaret married him simply from curiosity and weariness. Such an extreme statement cannot stand a moment against other evidence. It is clear that Margaret's husband was not literary or a scholar. She had doubtless seen quite enough of that sort of gentry in her varied career. But there is no doubt that he was a high-minded, dignified gentleman, and that he was devoted to her with an attachment which, coming from a temperament like his, is in itself strong testimony to the nobleness of her character. As for the ever-increasing depth of her regard for him, it is apparent whenever she mentions his name. She was nearly forty years old; she had been through a wide variety of emotional experiences; she knew the human heart, and here she had found one whose grave earnestness and loyal affection could be counted upon in every trial. "Simple, true, delicate, and retiring," she calls him, in well-weighed words, and adds, "while some of my friends have thought me exacting, Ossoli has outgone my expectations in the disinterestedness, the uncompromising bounty, of his every action." [67]

Then she became a mother, and yet one more profound chamber of her heart was opened. She had always loved children and had had a peculiar power of drawing their confidence, as that of their elders. She longed for motherhood, "my heart was too suffocated without a child of my own." [68] Yet she longed with an unusual and beautiful humility: "I am too rough and blurred an image of the Creator, to become a bestower of life." [69] When her son was born, she seemed almost to forget her existence in his. Her brain was all plans for rearing and guiding and helping him. His illness shakes her faith more than anything else had ever done before. His health and gayety make her gay when all is troubled around her.

For these strange, new experiences had come to her in a troubled world. Her husband was thickly concerned in the Italian revolution, and she herself gave all her natural ardor to the coming of a new era in the country she had loved and known so well. As battles were fought and men were wounded and suffering, she visited the hospitals, comforted the dying, cheered and tended the long and solitary hours of recovery. "A mild saint and ministering angel: that seems to have been the impression made by her at Rome upon those who knew her well,"[70] writes one friend. She shrinks at first: "I had no idea before, how terrible gunshot-wounds and wound-fever are";[71] but these tremors are instantly overcome, and she shows the same power over the cruder forms of human suffering that she had tendered to the wayward struggles of the spirit. "How long will the Signora stay? When will the Signora come again?"[72] was the eager murmur from the hearts she had cheered and comforted.

It will be asked, where was the old Margaret, the disagreeable Margaret, the harsh, dominating, self-willed egotism? Not wholly dead, doubtless. She herself says: "In the foundation of my character, in my

aims I am always the same." [73] So are we all. But
at least her heart had been immensely changed and
modified by love and pity. She had suffered in life
far more than she had enjoyed, she says, and suffering
changes all hearts one way or the other. Ambition?
She still cherishes it in a manner, still hopes to be a
great writer, plans a history of the noble doings in Italy,
which was lost with her, to the regret of many. Self-
culture, all the fine Goethean theories? Oh, perhaps she
has them, but she has at last come to know the great
secret, — that the height of self-culture is to forget
culture and to forget self; that he that loseth his
life shall find it. And in the pity of her struggle —
struggle with health, struggle with narrow circumstances, struggle with war and the ruins of war — her
courage almost ebbs away in a languishing cry: "Yes; I
am weary, and faith soars and sings no more. Nothing
is left good of me, except at the bottom of the heart a
melting tenderness." [74] Surely a strange utterance from
the haughty spirit of earlier years.

So the high Italian dream was over. There was nothing left for Margaret and her husband among his people,
and her thoughts turned again to home. She would
go back to America, would strive once more to gain
recognition of her powers, aiming rather at others'

profit than her own. She accepted the task, made such preparations as she could. But her heart was heavy, weighed down with undue, unreasonable fear. "I am become a miserable coward. I fear heat and cold and even mosquitoes. I fear terribly the voyage home, fear biting poverty." [75] Everything connected with her journey seemed to turn into sad omen, or so she read it in her doubting soul. At the very last moment the foreboding was so heavy that she found it difficult to force herself to go on board the vessel. She did so, and all her fears were realized. She passed the Atlantic safely, only to be wrecked on Fire Island beach in July, 1850. We need not analyze the extensive investigations and confused narratives of the final disaster. It is enough to know that Margaret perished with her husband and child, as she would have wished.

It was a pathetic, tragic end to a tragic career. We certainly cannot say that Margaret's life was wasted when we appreciate her immense influence upon her contemporaries and those who came after her. Yet it does not seem as if her achievement matched her powers. She was a woman of marvelous complexity, like all women, and all men, and her complexity strikes you with tenfold force because she went out like a candle when a window is suddenly opened into great night.

VI
LOUISA MAY ALCOTT

CHRONOLOGY

Louisa May Alcott.
Born in Germantown, Pennsylvania, November 29, 1832.
Grew up mainly in Concord and Boston.
Nursed in Washington hospitals, 1862–1863.
"Little Women" published October, 1868.
In Europe, 1865–1866 and 1870–1871.
Died March 6, 1888.

LOUISA MAY ALCOTT

VI

LOUISA MAY ALCOTT

I

Her father thought himself a philosopher. His family agreed with him. So did his friend and contemporary, Emerson, and a few others. He was at any rate a philosopher in his complete inability to earn or to keep money. Her mother was by nature a noble and charming woman, by profession a household drudge. Louisa and her three sisters were born in odd corners between 1830 and 1840 and grew up in Concord and elsewhere. They knew a little, quite enough, about philosophy and a great deal about drudgery. Louisa determined in early youth to eschew philosophy and drudgery both, to be independent, and to earn an honest livelihood for herself and her family. She did it, wrote books that charmed and paid, and died wornout before she was old, but with a comfortable lapful of glory.

I do not mean to imply that the Alcotts' poverty was sordid or pitiable. Innate dignity of character, sweetness and natural cheerfulness, kept it from being anything of the kind. If they had not money, they had high ideals; and high ideals afford a certain substitute for comfort, after they have thrust it out of doors. No doubt, also, the rugged discipline of privation fits souls better for the ups and downs of life, which, for most men and women, mean more hardship than comfort. At the same time, to understand Louisa Alcott, what she did and what she was, we must keep the bitterness of youthful poverty before us, the perpetual struggle to get clothes and food and other necessaries, the burden of debts and charity, the fret and strain of nerves worn with anxiety and endeavor, the endless uncertainty about the future. "It was characteristic of this family that they never were conquered by their surroundings,"[1] says the biographer. This is true; yet such experiences fray the edges of the soul, when they do not impair its substance. Louisa's soul was frayed. Poverty bit her like a north wind, spurred to effort, yet chilled and tortured just the same. "Little Lu began early to feel the family cares and peculiar trials,"[2] she says of her childhood. In her young-womanhood, when just beginning to see her way, she is hampered in the walks she likes because of "stockings with a profusion of toe, but no heel, and shoes with plenty of heel, but a paucity of toe."[3] Later still, when the world ought to have been going well with her, her cry is, "If I think of my woes

I fall into a vortex of debts, dishpans, and despondency awful to see." [4]

The nature of these troubles and the depth of them were specially evident to her, because she was born with a shrewd native wit and keen intelligence. Her education was somewhat erratic, furnished mainly by her father from his wide but heterogeneous store and with eccentric methods. From her childhood she was an impetuous reader, of all sorts of books and in all sorts of ways and places. She read stories and poems, and more serious writings, when the whim seized her. Goethe, for example, she liked early and praised late, though I do not know that much of Goethe is to be seen in her life or in her best-known books. Above all, she employed her brain for practical objects, loved mental method and tidiness. "I used to imagine my mind a room in confusion, and I was to put it in order; so I swept out useless thoughts and dusted foolish fancies away, and furnished it with good resolutions and began again. But cobwebs get in. I'm not a good housekeeper, and never get my room in nice order." [5] And with the same practical tendency she analyzed all things about her and all men and women. Her father's various contacts brought many people to his door, and Louisa learned early to distinguish. "A curious jumble of fools and philosophers," [6] she says calmly of one of his beloved clubs. No doubt she would have given the same verdict on the world in general and with the same wise caution as to deciding the proportions. Nor was she less ready to analyze herself, as portrayed in one of her stories. "Much describing of other people's passions and feelings set her to studying and speculating about her own — a morbid amusement, in which healthy young minds do not voluntarily indulge." [7]

What marked her character in all this was honesty, sincerity, straightforward simplicity. Like Jo in "Little Women," who follows her creatress so closely, Louisa, as a child, had more of the boy than of the girl about her, did not care for frills or flounces, did not care for dances or teas, liked fresh air and fresh thoughts and hearty quarrels and forgetful reconciliations. She would shake your hand and look in your eye and make you trust her. Jo's wild words were always getting her into scrapes. "Oh, my tongue, my abominable tongue! Why can't I learn to keep it quiet?" [8] So she sighed, and so Louisa had often sighed before her. But with the outspokenness went a splendid veracity and a loathing for what was false or mean or cowardly. "With all her imagination and romance, Miss Alcott was a tremendous destroyer of illusions," [9] says Mrs. Cheney;

"Oh, wicked L. M. A., who hates sham and loves a joke,"[10] says Miss Alcott herself.

The disposition to excessive analysis and great frankness in expressing the results of the same are not especially favorable to social popularity or success, and it does not appear that Louisa had these things or wished to have them. Here again Jo renders her creatress very faithfully. She was perfectly capable of having a jolly time in company; in fact, when she was in the mood and with those she liked, she could be full of fun and frolic, could lead everybody in wild laughter and joyous pranks and merriment. She could run into a party of strangers at the seashore and be gay with them. "Found a family of six pretty daughters, a pleasant mother, and a father who was an image of one of the Cheeryble brothers. Had a jolly time boating, driving, charading, dancing, and picnicking. One mild moonlight night a party of us camped out on Norman's Woe, and had a splendid time, lying on the rocks singing, talking, sleeping, and rioting up and down."[11] But usually she was shy with strangers, perhaps shyer with people she knew or half knew, had no patience with starched fashions or fine manners, liked quiet, old garments, old habits, and especially the society of her own soul. She complains that her sister "doesn't enjoy quiet corners as I do,"[12] and she complains further, through the mouth of Jo, that "it's easier for me to risk my life for a person than to be pleasant to him when I don't feel like it." [13]

With this disposition we might expect her to have a small list of friends, but those very near and dear. I do not find it so. "She did not encourage many intimacies," says Mrs. Cheney. Though reasonably indifferent to the conventions, she would not have inclined to keep up any especially confidential relations with men. As for women, she wrote of her younger days, "Never liked girls, or knew many, except my sisters." [14] If she did not make women friends in her youth, she was not likely to in age.

All her affection, all her personal devotion, seem to have been concentrated upon her family, and from childhood till death her relations with them were close and unbroken. How dearly she loved her sisters shines everywhere through the faithful family picture preserved in "Little Women," and the peculiar tenderness Jo gave to Beth is but an exact reflection of what the real Elizabeth received from the real Louisa. In "Little Women" the affection is made only more genuine by the trifling tiffs and jars which always occur in nature, if not always in books. So in Louisa's journal her admirable frankness carefully records an occasional freak or sparkle of irritation or jealously. "I feel very moral to-day, having done a big wash alone, baked, swept the house, picked the hops, got dinner, and written a chapter in 'Moods.' May gets exhausted with work, though she walks six miles without a murmur." [15] Again, of the same younger sister: "How different our lives are just now! — I so lonely, sad, and sick; she so happy, well and blest. She always had the cream of things, and deserved it. My time is yet to come somewhere else, when I am ready for it." [16] Perhaps the sympathy between Jo and Amy in the story was less complete than in the case of the older sisters. Yet the chief interest of Louisa's later years was her love for the child her sister May had left her.

For her father, as for her sisters, she cherished a devoted attachment. No doubt in this, as in the other, there were human flaws. At times she implies a gentle wish that he might have done a little more for the comfort of his family even if a little less for their eternal salvation. But this was momentary. Her usual attitude was one of tender and affectionate devotion, of entire and reverent appreciation of that pure and unworldly spirit. Emerson tells her that her father might have talked with Plato. [17] She is delighted and thinks of him as Plato and often calls him Plato afterward.

How admirable in its blending of elements is her picture of his return from one of his unprofitable wanderings: "His dress was neat and poor. He looked cold and thin as an icicle, but serene as God."[18] To her he was God in a manner, and with reasonable discounts.

But with her mother there seem to have been no discounts whatever. The affection between them was perfect and holy and enduring. Her mother understood her,—all her wild ways and lawless desires and weaknesses and untrimmed strength. It was to her mother that she turned in joy and trouble, and in both she never failed to find the response she looked for. After her mother's death she writes: "I never wish her back, but a great warmth seems gone out of life, and there is no motive to go on now."[19] Yet if there was nothing left to do, there was comfort in the thought of what she had done. For she was able to write, a few years before, "Had the pleasure of providing Marmee with many comforts, and keeping the hounds of care and debt from worrying her. She sits at rest in her sunny room, and that is better than any amount of fame to me."[20]

So we see that when Jo cried, in her enthusiastic fashion, "I do think that families are the most beautiful things in all the world!"[21] it was a simple transcript from nature. Also, it is most decidedly to be observed that Louisa's regard for her family was by no means mere sentiment, but a matter of strenuous practical effort. Indeed, it is not certain that the conscientious sense of duty is not even more prominent in her domestic relations than affection itself. "Duty's faithful child," [22] her father called her, and the faithfulness of her duty meant more to him and his than anything else in the world. I have dwelt already upon her poignant appreciation of the hardships and privations of her childhood. Though she bore these with reasonable patience, she early and constantly manifested a distinct determination to escape from them. "I wish I was rich, I was good, and we were all a happy family this day." [23] Note even here that the wish is general and that she wants to save them all from trials as well as herself. Her own comfort and ease she was ready to sacrifice and did sacrifice. Did May need a new bonnet? She should have it and Louisa would get on with a refurbished old one. Did money come in somewhat more freely? Louisa got mighty little of it herself. There were so many mouths to fill and clothes to buy and bills to pay. She would give anything and give up anything that she had to give or give up. The sacrifice of hair, which Jo accomplished with so many tears, was not actually achieved in Louisa's case, but she was ready to make it, — and who doubts that she would have made it?

Yet she did not relish sacrifice, or ugly things, or petty dependence. She was bound to get out of the rut she was born in; how, she did not care, so long as she did nothing dishonest or unworthy. Debts, — she certainly would not have debts; but comfort she would have and would pay for it. She would prove that "though an *Alcott* I *can* support myself."[24] When she was but a child she went out alone into the fields, and vowed with bitter energy: "I *will* do something by-and-by. Don't care what, teach, sew, act, write, anything to help the family; and I'll be rich and famous and happy before I die, see if I won't."[25]

II

It would be of course quite false to imply that Miss Alcott was a wholly practical, even mercenary, person, who lived and wrote for money only, or that the rugged experiences of her youth had crushed out of her sensibility and grace and imagination and all the varied responses which are supposed to constitute the artistic temperament. It is true, she had one artistic representative in her family, and the consciousness of old bonnets refurbished on that account may have somewhat re-

pressed the genial flow of æsthetic impulse in her own
character. But she had abundance of wayward emotion,
nevertheless, and if she subdued it in one form, it escaped in another. "Experiences go deep with me,"[26] she
said, and it was true. It does not appear that she had
any especial taste for the arts. Painting she refers to
occasionally with mild enthusiasm, music with little
more. Perhaps we cannot quite take the Lavinia of
"Shawl Straps" as autobiographical, but her journal
sounds uncommonly like Louisa: "Acres of pictures.
Like about six out of the lot:"[27] again, "I *am* glad to
have seen this classical cesspool (Rome), and still more
glad to have got out of it alive."[28] Nature appealed to
her, of course, as it must have done to the child of Concord and the worshiper of Emerson. Still, the rendering
of it in her writings, "Flower Stories," etc., and even
in the best of her poems, "Thoreau's Flute," cannot be
said to be profound. Her nature feeling is much more
attractive in the brief touches of her Journal: "I had an
early run in the woods before the dew was off the grass.
The moss was like velvet, and as I ran under the arches
of yellow and red leaves I sang for joy, my heart was so
bright and the world so beautiful."[29] Also, she had a
keen sense of the pleasant and graceful ornaments of
life, all the more keen because her childhood had been so

barren of such things. "How I wish I could be with you, enjoying what I have always longed for, — fine people, fine amusements, and fine books." [30] She liked these things, though she liked other things still more. "I love luxury, but freedom and independence better." [31]

Her sensibility and quick emotion showed, however, far less in artistic enjoyment than in the inner play and shifting movements of her own spirit. The sudden variety of nature she sees reflected in herself. "It was a mild, windy day, very like me in its fitful changes of sunshine and shade." [32] She was a creature of moods and fancies, smiles and tears, hopes and discouragements, as we all are, but more than most of us. From her childhood she liked to wander, had roaming limbs and a roaming soul. She "wanted to see every thing, do every thing, and go every where." [33] She loved movement, activity, boys' sports and boys' exercise: "I always thought I must have been a deer or a horse in some former state, because it was such a joy to run." [34] Then she got tired and got cross, and when she was young said bitter things and repented them, and when she grew older would have liked to say them and repented that also. And the ill-temper shifted suddenly and madly to laughter, merry drollery, wild sallies, quips, and teasing frolics, full well remembered by lovers of "Little

Women." "The jocosity of my nature will gush out when it gets a chance,"[35] she says.

Sometimes the same wild spirit would rise higher into a state of eager exhilaration and excitement. She longed for change, adventure, even suffering. She put melodrama into her stories; she would have liked to put it into her life. When the future seems peculiarly uncertain, she writes: "It's a queer way to live, but dramatic, and I rather like it; for we never know what is to come next."[36] And again follows the reaction and depression, as deep as the excitement was high and exhilarating, depression far more serious than mere superficial temper, seizing and shaking the root-fibers of the soul. In her more elaborate novels, "Moods" and "A Modern Mephistopheles," she has analyzed these spiritual variations, perhaps with some exaggeration, but with an evident autobiographical basis; and her heroine's miseries certainly reflect her own. Tears she does not often yield to, but when she weeps, she does it thoroughly: "As I seldom indulge in this moist misery, I like to enjoy it with all my might, when I do."[37]

Her active conscience prompts her to resist, to bear up against real trial and the still worse monotony of everyday care. There is an education for her in grief, she says; she must make the best of it and profit by it. There is a pleasure in drudgery, she says, if one can only find it. "A dull, heavy month, grubbing in the kitchen, sewing, cleaning house, and trying to like my duty." [38] But she doesn't like it, and it wears, and the immortal spirit loses its lightness and its freshness and is almost ready to give up the fight: "So every day is a battle, and I'm so tired I don't want to live; only it's cowardly to die till you have done something." [39] Even, on one dark day, all further struggle came to seem impossible, and as she passed the running tide on her way to Boston, she almost made up her mind not to pass it. But she did, and her "fit of despair was soon over . . . and I went home resolved to take Fate by the throat and shake a living out of her." [40] Afterwards the little experience served to make a story, as it has done for other writers and sufferers.

It will be asked how far matters of the heart entered into these depressions and despairs in Miss Alcott's case. Directly, not very much. It is true that in the story just referred to she suggests love or the lack of it as the exciting cause for suicide. "It is not always want, insanity, or sin that drives women to desperate deaths; often it is a dreadful loneliness of heart, a hunger for home and friends, worse than starvation, a bitter sense of wrong in being denied the tender ties, the pleasant duties, the sweet rewards that can make the humblest life happy." [41] But there is no indication that, in her own case, any disappointed love, any ungratified longing, was added to the otherwise sufficient cares that weighed down her mercurial spirit. Though the story of Jo is so largely autobiographical, the marriage to Professor Bhaer, in itself not exceptionally romantic, is pure invention, and there is nothing else to show that Louisa's heart was ever seriously touched. She had at least one offer of marriage, and considered accepting it as another form of self-sacrifice for the benefit of her suffering family.[42] From this, even more disastrous than the projected tonsorial martyrdom, she was happily dissuaded; and if other similar opportunities occurred, they are not mentioned.

She would even have us believe — and so would her biographer — that she took little interest in love matters and introduced them in her books for purposes of sale and popular success. "She always said that she got tired of everybody," says Mrs. Cheney, "and felt sure that she should of her husband if she married." [43] Miss Alcott herself expresses some interest in possible children of her own and a certain admiration for babies, but she has observed that few marriages are happy ones [44] and she thinks that "liberty is a better husband than love to many of us." [45]

This may be all very true. Nevertheless, it will hardly. be denied that many of her stories reek with amorousness. Perhaps this was precisely because the subject did not naturally interest her, and, being anxious to deal with it enough to please the public and make money, she dealt with it too much. But the explanation seems rather far-fetched, and I am inclined to believe that she had all a woman's interest in lovers, whatever may have been her opinion of husbands. Her references to personal appearance, both her own and others', show a due sensitiveness to natural charms and to their possible appeal to the other sex. If she looks in the glass, she tries "to keep down vanity about my long hair, my well-shaped head, and my good nose," [46] but she is sufficiently aware of their attraction, all the same. Indeed, in her vicarious love-making there is a curious, teasing insistence that suggests far more than a mere mercenary preoccupation; and in the serious novels, into which she put her best artistic effort, the almost feverish eroticism would seem to indicate, as with other unmarried writers, a constant presence of the woman in her extreme femininity, however obscure and unacknowledged.

As Miss Alcott had all the sensitiveness, the whims and shifts of mood, the eccentric possibilities, of the born artist, so she was by no means without the artist's

instinct of ambition and desire for fame. From childhood she wanted to do something that would make her
great and distinguished and a figure in the mouths and
hearts of men. She wanted to act; wrote plays and pro-
duced them in the parlor, as Jo did; had visions of oper-
atic and theatrical triumphs. She envied the successes
of great authors. When she read " Jane Eyre," she
writes: " I can't be a C. B., but I may do a little something
yet." [47] Her young friends tease her about being an
authoress. She assures them that she will be, though
she adds modestly to herself, " Will if I can, but something else may be better for me." [48] Not only has she
the theory of authorship, but all her emotions and desires
and fancies naturally seek literary expression. When
she was a child, she wrote verses for the pure delight of
it, — not great verses certainly, but they pleased and re-
lieved her. When she stood at the other extreme of life,
she wrote verses still. " Father and I cannot sleep, but
he and I make verses as we did when Marmee died." [49]
When she was weary or overwrought, she turned to
her pen for distraction, if not for comfort. " Began
a book called ' Genius.' Shall never finish it, I dare say,
but must keep a vent for my fancies to escape at." [50]

She viewed life from the artist's angle also, took it
impersonally in its larger relations as well as in its imme-

diate appeal to her. She notes early in her Journal that she began to see the strong contrasts and the fun and follies in every-day life. She always saw them and always had the strong impulse to turn them into literature. And her methods were not mechanical, did not savor of the shop or the workbench. In the interesting account of them which she jotted down in later years the marked flavor of inspiration and artistic instinct is apparent. She never had a study, she says, writes with any pen or paper that come to hand, always has a head full of plots and a heart full of passions, works them over at odd moments and writes them down from memory, as fancy and convenience dictate. Quiet she wants, and solitude, if possible, and a stimulating environment, or at least not a deadening one. "Very few stories written in Concord; no inspiration in that dull place. Go to Boston, hire a quiet room and shut myself in it." [51]

If the creative impulse possesses her, it possesses her wholly. When she *can* work, she *can't* wait, she says. Sleep is of no consequence, food is of no consequence. She can't work slowly. The ideas boil and bubble and must find their vent. When she was writing her favorite "Moods," there was no rest for her. She was tied to her desk day after day. Her family alternately praised and worried. Her mother administered tea and her father red apples. "All sorts of fun was going on; but I did n't care if the world returned to chaos if I and my inkstand only 'lit' in the same place."[52] Then, after the excitement of labor came the excitement of glory. Men and women, well known in her world at any rate, crowded to praise and compliment. "I liked it, but think a small dose quite as much as is good for me; for after sitting in a corner and grubbing *à la* Cinderella, it rather turns one's head to be taken out and be treated like a princess all of a sudden."[53]

Nor did she lack the discouragement and depression inseparable from all artistic effort. There were the endless external difficulties which every artist knows and none but artists much sympathize with: the frets, the home cares, always so much accentuated in the case of a woman, even when she is unmarried, the perpetual, the trivial, and more harassing because trivial, interruptions. Idle neighbors chat of idle doings; hours slip away; when at last the free hour and the quiet spot are found, weary nerves have no longer any inspiration left in them. Of one of her books that she loved she says pathetically: "Not what it should be, — too many interruptions. Should like to do one book in peace, and see if it would n't be good."[54] On another occasion she gets ready for a fit of work. Then John Brown's daughters come to board; arrangements have to be made for them and their comfort provided for. Louisa cries out her sorrow on the fat ragbag in the garret and sets to work at housekeeping. "I think disappointment must be good for me, I get so much of it; and the constant thumping Fate gives me may be a mellowing process; so I shall be a ripe and sweet old pippin before I die."[55]

Yet the books get done somehow. Only, when they are done, the troubles seem just begun rather than ended. Publishers are refractory, such being their nature, like that of other human beings. Stories are accepted and all seems triumphant. But they do not come out; instead, are held back by long and quite needless delays, till it is evident that the world is criminally indifferent to works that are bound to be immortal. "All very aggravating to a young woman with one dollar, no bonnet, half a gown, and a discontented mind."[56]

Perhaps worst of all, when you do achieve success and are read and admired, there comes the deadly doubt about the value of your own work; for, however much they may resent the faultfinding of others, authors who really count are their own severest critics; and of all the sorrows of the literary life none is keener than the feeling that what you have done is far enough from what you would have liked to do. In this point, also, Miss

Alcott was an author, and she often indicates what she expressed freely in regard to some of her minor works. "They were not good, and though they sold the paper I was heartily ashamed of them . . . I'm glad of the lesson, and hope it will do me good." [57]

So we may safely conclude that it was not only hard necessity that drove her to write, but that if she had grown up in all comfort and with abundant means always at her command, she would still have felt the teasing impulses of the literary instinct, still have bound herself to the staid drudgery of ink and paper and been slave to the high hopes and deep despairs which mean life — and death — to those who are born with the curious longing to create things beautiful.

III

As it was, however, there can be no doubt that the solid need of earning money was the chief and enduring spur of her literary effort. She was not essentially and first of all a preacher, as was Mrs. Stowe. Some may disagree about this, considering the extreme moralizing of many, not to say all, of her stories. The moralizing is evident and undeniable. She not only took pains to avoid what might be, in her opinion, distinctly injurious, though there are critics who hold that in this she was far from successful; but she rarely misses an opportunity for direct preaching. Indeed, in some of her inferior writings the preaching is so overdone that it surfeits even her most ardent admirers. She is determined to preach, will not be hindered from preaching; boys and girls must learn something good, if they are to linger with her. Yet the fury of the effort implies something artificial about it. Her preaching is an acquired habit and discipline, not an inherited, divine impulse, like Mrs. Stowe's. When you look carefully into Louisa's religion, you appreciate at once what I mean. It was a sturdy, working religion, solid, substantial, full of good deeds and kindness. Her own hard experience had made her eminently ready to help others. When she gets money, she gives it, and she gives sympathy always. "I like to help the class of 'silent poor' to which we belonged for so many years."[58] But her own hard experience had been too closely connected with abstract religion and concrete philosophers for her to cherish much personal affection for abstract religion and philosophy. In her thoughtful childhood she did indeed touch God under the whisper of the great pines: "It seemed as if I *felt* God as I never did before, and I prayed in my heart that I might keep that happy sense of near-

ness all my life." [59]   But she was too honest to pay
herself with words, and to her, as to so many of her
contemporaries, religious hope remained simply a glim-
mering star to distract thought from dark gulfs that had
no hope in them at all. "Life always was a puzzle to
me, and gets more mysterious as I go on. I shall find it
out by and by and see that it's all right, if I can only
keep brave and patient to the end." [60]

Meantime she must earn money. She set out with
that motive in her youth and it abode with her till her
death. Do not take this in any sordid sense. She was as
far as possible from being a miser or a squanderer. She
found no pleasure in the long accumulation of a fortune,
none in the mad spending of it. But the terrible lack of
dollars in her childhood had taught her their value. All
her life she was in need of moderate ease herself and
those she loved needed it far more. Therefore she must
and she would and she did earn money. How she earned
it was of less importance, and she was perfectly ready
to try any of the few forms of earning then accessible
to women. "Tried for teaching, sewing, or any honest
work. Won't go home to sit idle while I have a head and
pair of hands." [61]   She takes a place as governess and
goes into ecstasy over her small wages: "Every one of
those dollars cried aloud, 'What, ho! Come hither, and

be happy!'"[62]   She even goes out as a simple servant, with disastrous results, as fully related by herself. Teaching comes into the list, of course. But she was never successful at it, and when Fields, with all a publisher's hearty kindness, says to her, "Stick to your teaching; you can't write," she murmurs, under her breath, "I won't teach; and I can write, and I'll prove it."[63]

For, of all the forms of drudgery for money, she found literature the most acceptable and agreeable. "I can't do much with my hands; so I will make a battering-ram of my head and make a way through this rough-and-tumble world."[64]   She did it; but do not imagine that the way was easy, that the dollars rolled into her lap, or that she could escape many hard knocks and staggering buffets. Late in her life a young man asked her if she would advise him to devote himself to authorship. "Not if you can do anything else, even dig ditches,"[65] was the bitter answer. For years she found the upward road a piece of long and tedious traveling. Hours had to be snatched where possible, or impossible, necessary tasks had to be slighted, health had to be risked and wasted, all to write stories which she knew to be worthless, but which she hoped would sell. They did sell after a fashion, brought her five dollars here, ten dollars there, enough to buy a pair of shoes or stop a gaping creditor's mouth for a moment. But what vast labor was expended for petty results or none, what vaster hopes were daily thrown down, only to be built up again with inexhaustible endurance and energy!

Even when success came and the five dollars were transformed into fifty and five hundred, there was struggle still, perhaps more wearing than at first. Engagements had to be met and publishers satisfied, no matter how irksome the effort. "I wrote it with left hand in a sling, one foot up, head aching, and no voice,"[66] she says of one story. Though money was abundant, it was never abundant enough: "The family seem so panic-stricken and helpless when I break down, that I try to keep the mill going."[67] To be sure, there was glory. When it began to come, she appreciated it keenly. "Success has gone to my head, and I wander a little. Twenty-seven years old, and very happy."[68] It was pleasant to be widely praised and admired, pleasant to have compliments from great men and brilliant women, pleasantest of all, perhaps, to feel that children loved your books and cried over them and loved you. Yet she seems to have felt the annoyances of glory more than most authors and to have savored its sweets less. Perhaps this was because she was early worn out with over-work and over-anxiety. "When I had the youth I had no money; now I have the money I have no time; and when I get the time, if I ever do, I shall have no health to enjoy life."[69] Fame bothered her. She resented the intrusions of reporters, even the kindly curiosity of adoring readers. What right had they to pester a quiet woman earning her living with desperate effort in her own way? For the earning, after all, was the side that appealed to her, the earning with all it meant. "The cream of the joke is, that we made our own money ourselves, and no one gave us a blessed penny. That does soothe my rumpled soul so much that the glory is not worth thinking of."[70]

Also, to be sure, she had always the feeling that she was not doing the best she could and that the money came most freely for the things she was not most proud of. In her early days she wrote and sold sensational stories of a rather cheap order. Certain features of these pleased her. She confesses quite frankly that she had "a taste for ghastliness"[71] and that she was "fond of the night side of nature."[72] But she longed to do something else, and she tried to, — in "Moods" and "A Modern Mephistopheles," — perhaps not very well, at any rate not very successfully. Few get the glory they want, but there is probably a peculiar bitterness in getting the glory you don't want.

Then she hit on a line of work which, if not great or original, was sane and genuine. She put her own life, her own heart into her books, and they were read with delight because her heart was like the hearts of all of us. As a child, she wanted to sell her hair to support her family. When she was older, she supported them by selling her flesh and blood, and theirs, but always with a fine and dignified reserve as well as a charming frankness. Every creative author builds his books out of his own experience. They would be worthless otherwise. But few have drawn upon the fund more extensively and constantly than Miss Alcott. And she was wise to do it, and when she ceased to do it, she failed. She could allege the great authority of Goethe for her practice: "Goethe puts his joys and sorrows into poems; I turn my adventures into bread and butter."[73] She could also have alleged the shrewdness and vast human experience of Voltaire, who said: "Whoever has, as you have, imagination and common-sense, can find in himself, without other aid, the complete knowledge of human nature."[74]

So she coined her soul to pad her purse and, incidentally, to give solace to many. The worshipers of art for art's sake may sneer at her, but she remains in excellent company. Scott, Dumas, Trollope, to name no others, collected cash, as well as glory, with broad and easy negligence. And the point is that, while doing so, they established themselves securely among the benefactors of mankind. The great thinkers, the great poets, the great statesmen, the great religious teachers sway us upward for our good. But they often lead us astray and they always harass us in the process. I do not know that they deserve much more of our gratitude than those who make our souls forget by telling charming stories. Perhaps "Little Women" does not belong in quite the same order as "Rob Roy," or "Les Trois Mousquetaires," or even "Phineas Finn." But it is not an unenviable fate to have gained an honest independence by giving profit and delight to millions. Miss Alcott did it—and Shakespeare.

VII
FRANCES ELIZABETH WILLARD

CHRONOLOGY

Frances Elizabeth Willard

Born in Churchville, New York, September 28, 1839.

Removed to Oberlin, Ohio, 1841.

Removed to Wisconsin, 1846.

At Milwaukee Female College, 1857.

At Northwestern Female College, 1858, 1859.

Taught till 1874.

Entered Temperance Work, 1874.

President National Woman's Christian Temperance Union, 1879.

President World's Woman's Christian Temperance Union, 1888.

Died February 17, 1898.

FRANCES WILLARD

FRANCES ELIZABETH WILLARD

I

SHE had the great West behind her; its sky and its distances, its fresh vigor and its unexampled joy. Her father carried his New England traditions and his infant children from New York in the early forties, — first to Ohio, then to Wisconsin, — and Frances and her brother and sister were fed full on corn, pork, farming, and religion. She herself cites with entire approval her mother's analysis of the child's fortunate heredity: "The Thompson generosity, the Willard delicacy, the Hill purpose and steadfastness, the French element coming from the Lewis family, make up an unique human amalgam."[1] Whatever her heredity, she had a sane and healthy childhood. She lived with the animals, and raced and romped and rioted; she lived with the Bible and with high ideals and direct and pointed English, and she contracted an abhorrence of whiskey which supplied her for life with a more eager stimulant than whiskey could possibly have furnished.

As a consequence of her breeding and surroundings,

she had excellent health. Her mother said that in childhood Frances was the most delicate of all her children and that she had an organism exceptionally susceptible to physical pain.[2] She herself enlarges often upon the exquisite fineness of her sensibility.[3] But fresh air, exercise, and ample sleep, maintained under even the greatest pressure of business, gave her a sound and vigorous body, and no doubt as much as anything else enabled her to say, near the very end of her career: "The chief wonder of my life is that I dare to have so good a time, both physically, mentally, and religiously."[4] To have so good a time, remember it.

With the well-nourished body and the firm, sturdy muscles went an unfailing energy of purpose and of execution. She was no listless performer of household duty, no tame dishwasher or bedmaker, doing routine tasks from day to day, without a thought beyond them. Her mother says: "I wonder sometimes that I had the wit to let her do what she preferred instead of obliging her to take up housework as did all the other girls of our acquaintance."[5] Wit or not, it was a course admirably suited to Frances. She dodged the dishpan, milked the cows instead, rode the horses, rode the cows, too, if the whim seized her, held the plough at need, and in the intervals roved the fields and pastures, and let her soul rove even more widely than her feet did. Routine of all sorts she hated always, and shunned it when she could. "To be tied to a bell rope," she says, was "an asphyxiating process from which I vainly sought escape, changing the spot only to keep the pain."[6]

Everything in her case, you see, favored the building up of a strong individuality, an ardent, independent will, and such was the result. She knew her own way and sought it with tremendous persistence and astonishing success. She had a spice of temper, which she well recognized and fought and got the better of, but with immense struggle. When she was a schoolgirl, she had an amiable playmate whose amiability irritated her. She "just stepped on Effie's toes at recess to see if she wouldn't frown, and sure enough she didn't."[7] All through life she felt an inclination to step on such amiable toes. Her willfulness showed in the inclination and her will in keeping it under.

Souls of this positive, individual temper are not always successful in their relations with others, do not always care to mingle with others or to frame their lives in conjunction with their fellow men and women. Miss Willard's account of herself shows strong symptoms of this self-withdrawing disposition. She speaks of her painful shyness in youth, of her difficulties in meeting people and in adapting herself to them. She makes an interesting admission, also, which places her sharply in one of the two great classes into which social humanity is divided: "I have an unconquerable aversion to intercourse with my superiors in position, age, or education."[8] Such an aversion, like its opposite, is the key to many lives and furnishes a great help for understanding Miss Willard's.

On the other hand, she had many striking social qualities. Her rush and furious abundance of spirits, her immense mental activity, naturally sought utterance with those who would understand her and appreciate her ardor. She had varied and sparkling wit, could tell excellent stories and did, — stories that were remembered and repeated after her. She shone in conversation, — real conversation apparently, that is, in which others did their part as well as she. Her comment upon Emerson's well-known saying, "we descend to meet," is curious. She thinks that Emerson lived too early to know what true meeting was, and that the intercourse of advanced, emancipated women almost realizes the privileges of celestial society.[9] Yet in a milder moment she herself admits that wholly successful conversation is possible only with the very limited number who are akin to us. If she who had talked with thousands and thousands could write the following words, surely there is some excuse for those who find life a spiritual solitude. "I do not believe that six persons have ever heard me talk, and not more than three ever in private converse heard my *vox humana,* simply because they were not skilled musicians. . . . For myself I know so little of [perfect response] that only as a foretaste of heaven's companionships do I think of such beatitude at all." [10]

However unsatisfactory Miss Willard may have found general society, there is no question as to her deep tenderness for her intimate friends and fellow workers. In her "Autobiography" she gives a curious analysis of the passionate affections of her girlhood. They were marked by all the sensitiveness, all the confidence, all the jealousy of woman's love for man. In the letters written in later years to one of her co-laborers I find much the same tone of devoted personal attachment: "I would I could fondly believe myself one tithe as much a woman after your own heart, as you are after mine. I don't mean to let you go your gait away from my ken and kindly regards 'never no more.'" [11]

Above all, from youth to age, Miss Willard felt this yearning, clinging affection for the members of her own family. Her father and brother were very dear to her. Her sister, Mary, whose brief life she commemorated in the little volume entitled, "Nineteen Beautiful Years," was even dearer. When she first parted from them, the wrench shook her whole being, and she describes the pain of it in delightfully characteristic language: "I have cried like a child, no, like a strong man, rather, until I quivered with trying to suppress the sobs that would make themselves audible."[12] With her mother the relation was closest of all. Mrs. Willard reared her daughter to be a notable woman, made her worthy to be so, and lived to see her so, with infinite satisfaction. And Frances's admiration and adoration for her mother continued and increased through life. "My nature is so woven into hers that I almost think it would be death for me to have the bond severed and one so much myself gone over the river."[13]

And how about men? It is evident enough that such a vivid, passionate nature had treasures of affection to bestow, if circumstances had favored it. She had lovers, too. At least she says so, and I believe her. In the bitter, slightly over-bitter, analysis which she makes of herself, she says that she is "not beautiful, pretty, or even good-looking."[14] Others thought differently, and one enthusiast concluded from her appearance in age that in youth she "must have possessed a rare and exquisite beauty." [15] However this may be, I fancy she was liked even more for her words and spirit than for her looks. She implies that possibly, if the right man had wooed her, she might have been won. The right man never did. Meantime, her comments upon love and her own capacity for love and her rigid resistance to love are delicious. I wish I could quote the whole of them. "I have never been in love, I have never shed a tear or dreamed a dream, or sighed, or had a sleepless hour for love. . . . I was too cautious, loved my own peace too well, valued myself too highly, re-membered too frequently that I was made for something far more worthy than to spend a disconsolate life, wast-ing my heart, the richest gift I could bestow, upon a man who did not care for it." [16] This when she was but little over twenty. Many years later she adds: "Of the real romance of my life, unguessed save by a trio of close friends, these pages may not tell." [17] Oh, but I wish they might have told! What would she have said of the love she had, when she writes so ardently of the love she had not!

But love in her career was a mere phantom, a drift-ing rose-cloud. She had other things to think of that were, or seemed to her, more important. And what apparatus and equipment had she for thinking of them? She had a good background of intelligence and thought behind her, came of New England stock that was accustomed to deal with the abstract problems of life, as well as with the practical. She had a substantial and fairly varied education. She read very widely, even in her younger days. When she was eighteen, she placidly informed her father that, being of age, she was going to read novels, though he disapproved of them.[18] She did. The list of books on her desk when she was twenty is portentous: Watts "On the Mind," Kames's "Elements of Criticism," Niebuhr's "Life and Letters,"[19] etc. She was brought up on Lord Chesterfield's letters to his son and tried to put his precepts into practice. She digested the disillusioned maxims of Chamfort and quotes with approval one of the most disillusioned of them: "In great matters men show themselves as they wish to be seen; in small matters as they are."[20]

And she had the natural thinking power, without which books, even disillusioned, obscure the spirit's progress rather than help it. She made up her mind about things independently, made it up quickly, made it up firmly, though she always recognized the possibility of change with a changing point of view. "This

is my opinion now; will it change? It may seem wrong
to others. It is *my* way of thinking, and I have a right
to it. That right I will maintain." [21]   She analyzed
everything fearlessly, — analyzed her own heart, analyzed nature and the world, analyzed the men and
women about her. Her analysis may not always have
been perfect or profound. It was at least sincere, and,
on the whole, free from prejudice. She analyzed life,
and especially, with curious force and bareness, she
analyzed death. How simple and direct is the account
in her Journal of her feelings at the bedside of her
dying sister: "I leaned on the railing at the foot of
the bed and looked at my sister— my sister Mary—
and knew that she was dead, knew that she was alive!
Everything was far off; I was benumbed and am but
waking to the tingling agony." [22]   How vivid and poignant are the reflections suggested by the same scene
in regard to herself: "Then, too, I am coming right
straight on to the same doom: I, who sit here this bright
morning, with carefully made toilet, attentive eyes, ears
open to every sound, I, with my thousand thoughts, my
steady-beating heart, shall lie there so still, so cold, and
for so long." [23]

If she applied such analysis to everything, and from
her early childhood, how was it with religion, — when

did it take hold of her, how fully, how genuinely, how deeply? Her sensibility was keen enough to be much stirred by its emotional side. She was sensitive to everything. Art indeed did not come within her youthful range, and in later life she was too busy for it. But music she loved and felt, and music as the expression of religious feeling had an almost overpowering effect on her. The sense of mystery was present with her, too, always, even in the midst of common things: "I have the feeling of one who walks blindfold among scenes too awful for his nerves to bear, in the midst of which we eat and drink, wash our faces and complain that the fire won't burn in the grate, or that the tea-bell does n't ring in season." [24] But in early days her analytical temper reacted against religion as against other things. The letter of doubt and questioning which she wrote to her teacher in the midst of a revival, with its unconscious reproduction of a wicked jest of Voltaire, — "O God, if there be a God, save my soul, if I have a soul," [25] — is a curious document. Nevertheless, she later accepted the orthodox faith in full and with complete, though always enlightened, abandonment. Only religion to her was action, — doing something for somebody, not dreaming or theological speculation. Her creed was broad enough to take in the whole world, but its essence was practice. In other words, her religion was not a science, but an art, the art she meant when one of her friends complained, "How can you think it right to give up your interest in literature and art?" and Miss Willard answered, "What greater art than to try to restore the image of God to faces that have lost it?" [26]

II

For she was above all, and more than all, a worker for humanity, and it as such that the study of her character becomes profoundly interesting. Let us first consider her work objectively, as it were, that is, in its effect upon others, and then in its even more interesting effect upon herself. From a child she wanted to do something in the world, to make men happier and better and fitter for this life and for another. She realized intensely the miseries of existence, those unavoidable and those that might so easily be avoided. She heard the cries of suffering that all might hear, and her vivid imagination pictured the cries that were heard of none. "I wish my mission might be to those who make no sign, yet suffer most intensely under their cold, impassive faces." [27] All through her youth she was restless, eager, longing, yet knew not what to do more than the

daily task that came in her way. Then the temperance
cause called her, with suffrage and the general advancement of women as adjuncts. She had found what she
wanted and she worked for it till death, with every
power that was in her. Thought of personal profit there
was none; we may say it with absolute certainty. She
liked comfort and she spent with freedom, but when
she declares "I'll never lay up money and I'll never be
rich,"[28] we know it is true.

And what admirable powers she had for the work!
Energy? Her energy was inexhaustible, and as well
directed as it was tireless. She herself tells us so: "I
have never been discouraged, but ready on the instant
with my decision, and rejoicing in nothing so much as
the taking of initiatives."[29] But we know it without
her telling us. Labor? She can labor like a machine.
"What it would be to have an idle hour I find it hard
to fancy."[30] She was careful as to sleep and regular
as to exercise, but beyond that every minute was util-
ized. She traveled scores of thousands of miles, spoke
often several times a day, answered every letter, some
twenty thousand a year.[31] She wasted no strength in
worry or regret over lost opportunities. All the thought
she gave to failure was to learn from it. "If it be
ambitious to have no fear of failure in any undertak-

ing, to that I must plead guilty. . . . I frankly own that no position I have ever attained gave me a single perturbed or wakeful thought, nor could any that I would accept." [32]

Other gifts besides effort are needed, however, to ensure the triumph of a great cause. Whatever they may be, Miss Willard had them. There is the gift of organization, of combining great bodies of men and women together for a clearly defined purpose and making them work in unison till that purpose is achieved. When she was a child, she devised clubs and framed elaborate constitutions for them. When she became a woman, she did the same work, efficiently, rapidly, and with eminent success.

And there is the gift of speech. So many great ideas and noble conceptions are lost in realization because the initiators of them cannot put them into adequate words and fire the world; just as a fluent and admirable power of the tongue is too often given to those who have nothing behind it. Miss Willard's tongue had assuredly something behind it; but her power of expression was always ample, adequate, and either seductive or commanding, as she wished. She herself knew well what this gift of eloquence was, and used it to the full, and cultivated it. "The spoken word, with a life and character back of it, the spoken word, sped home by earnest voice, conversational tone, and punctuating gesture, is the final human factor in the progress of reform."[33] Yet all testimony shows that her speeches were not oratorical, not rhetorical, not stuffed with formal figures or pompous trumpery. She went right to the heart, spoke as if her hearers were friends or brothers and sisters, unveiled her own feelings and experiences as if she were chatting at the fireside. "That was the most homey talk I ever heard,"[34] said an old farmer, after listening to her with tears.

This quality of simplicity in her public utterance was immensely emphasized by her appearance and manner. There was nothing imposing or dominating about her; rather an impression of frankness, gentleness, sympathetic and insinuating grace. One of her admirers, in endeavoring to describe her, says that her features refuse "to be impressed separately in your memory. Only her smile and voice abide. She envelops you, permeates you, enfolds you."[35] The general suggestion of grace, of graciousness, recurs and is reiterated in all attempts to reproduce her charm.

For she did charm. She charmed multitudes from the platform, made them, for the time at least, anxious to carry out her ideas and do her bidding. She charmed

individuals, took them in quiet corners and whispered
to them some spell of conviction which sent them out
into the world to try to make life over, as she would
have it.   She entered into other peoples' souls, put herself in their places, saw the world as they saw it.   There
was a certain amount of theory about this attitude on
her part.   Tact, adaptation, adjustment, were all a matter of principle with her.   For a child to have been
brought up on the "Letters of Lord Chesterfield"[36] was
no bad preparation for meeting the world, though one
is rather surprised to find it on a Wisconsin farm.   She
preaches deference, courtesy, and consideration to
everybody, no matter what their position in life.   "Who
says kind words to the man that blacks his boots, to
the maid that makes his bed and sweeps his hearth? . . .
Oh, we forget these things!"[37]   But with Miss Willard
there was more to it than theory.   She was interested
in the lives of all men and women, curious about them.
"I am somewhat of a questioner,"[38] she says.   She
questioned everybody, and so got a peep into the heart.
But back of the questioning were tenderness and sympathy and kindness, the desire not only to understand
but to help, not only to analyze but to make over.   And
precisely in this combination of understanding with love
lay her mighty power over men, the infinite tact which

enabled her to identify other wills with her own and so to persuade rather than to command for the achievement of a great purpose.

Even in her early days of teaching she formulated clearly the method that later obtained such vast results: "When you get them all to think alike and act alike by your command, you can do with them what you will."[39] But I prefer the testimony of a simple heart, which elucidates the whole point: "A poor seamstress said the other day: 'I go to sew at Miss Willard's sometimes. I see very little of her, scarcely hear her speak, but why is it I always leave there saying to myself: "I must be a better woman, I must indeed."'"[40] So the world said, when Miss Willard had done with it.

This is not the place to attempt more than to summarize briefly what the fullness of Miss Willard's actual achievement was. It may be that her ardent admirers somewhat exaggerate it, as is natural. To say that in her work for American women "she has done more to enlarge our sympathies, widen our outlook, and develop our gifts, than any man, or any other woman of her time,"[41] is making a broad claim, though perhaps not too broad. It is, at any rate, certain that, as head of the Woman's Christian Temperance Union, she diminished almost incalculably the sum of human misery, and

ways most curious to consider, and few have been exposed to the influence more overwhelmingly than Miss Willard.

The platform instinct was born in her. At three or four years old she was set up on a chair to recite hymns, and enjoyed it. Of one favorite she says: "Mother taught me how to speak it, where to put in the volume of sound and the soft, repressed utterance, and as for the pathos I knew where to put that in myself." [45] She always knew. And this instinct is not one that loses anything with the process of time. As years went on, publicity became existence to her; she thought in public, as it were, and all her inner life was lived in the presence of her faithful followers. Do not take this as in any way contradicting what I have said above about her charm and about her simplicity. There is no incompatibility here. It was just because life in public was so natural and easy to her, because she faced it without shrinking and without embarrassment, that she was able to convey herself, all her enthusiasms and ideals, so directly to others. The stimulus of a crowd roused her to intenser thought and feeling, just as one sympathetic auditor rouses others of a different temperament. To her, vast numbers were just one sympathetic auditor. Hear how shrewd and vivid is her own statement of this: "To me an audience is like a well-bred person, quiet, attentive, sympathetic, and, best of all, not in a position to answer back." [46]

And, as she felt the stimulus of an audience when it was before her, so she gradually came to carry one always in her mind, to feel that she was living before the vast audience of the world, and to put into every action the consciousness that it must be a lesson and an example. An amiable hostess thoughtlessly invites her to take a glass of wine when much fatigued. "The blood flushed in cheek and brow as I said to her, 'Madam, two hundred thousand women would lose somewhat of their faith in humanity if I should drink a drop of wine.'" [47] Think what it must be to feel the eyes of two hundred thousand women fixed upon you from the time you wake till the time you sleep again. This is the way Miss Willard lived.

Perhaps the most curious illustration of the sense of exemplariness is her "Autobiography." Here is a book of seven hundred closely printed pages, written by herself about herself, to be given to the world in her own lifetime, and the publishers inform us frankly that she originally wrote twelve hundred pages that had to be cut down. Assuredly no one ever turned themselves inside out more absolutely for the improvement of a hearkening world. And everywhere the necessity of setting an example is apparent. This becomes evident at once, when you compare the simple, natural journals of Miss Willard's youth with the carefully prepared matter of the later narrative. Of course nothing is false, nothing is misrepresented. Yet the consciousness of edification, the overwhelming nearness of the lecture platform, are everywhere present.

Now let us analyze a little more fully the effect of this curious life upon the woman's soul. To begin with, in the immense work she had undertaken of making over the world by the power of speech, did she experience alternations of hope and despair, enthusiasm and discouragement? Most men, and especially most women, one would think, would have had their hours of being exalted with the assured confidence of success, and hours again when blank depression would have made it seem as if they were beating at a stone wall. Symptoms of such depression may perhaps be detected in Miss Willard's " Autobiography," but I have looked for them curiously and I have found but few indeed. She had splendid health, she had an even temper, and she had an unfailing faculty of hope. If she had dark moments, she concealed them, perhaps out of consideration for the two hundred thousand.

I have also enjoyed probing the personal motives that lay behind her tremendous and constant effort, for she herself, in the seven hundred close pages, has invited such probing too earnestly for any one to resist it. We have already seen that she aimed to help mankind, — set out to do a noble work in the world, no doubt mainly for the sake of doing it. Her one sole aim, says her enthusiastic biographer, "has been to do the will of God as far as she knew it." [48] But to talk of the sole aim of any one is perilous. We are not made so neatly of one piece. Besides her large philanthropy, Miss Willard had a lot of healthy human ambition, just plain common desire to be admired and spoken well of and generally famous. She admits this herself very freely. "I have been called ambitious, and so I am, if to have had from childhood the sense of being born to a fate is an element of ambition." [49] She was keenly anxious to help on such fate also. In confessing her faults, she enumerates: "My chief besetments were, as I thought, a speculative mind, a hasty temper, a too ready tongue, and the purpose to be a celebrated person." [50] She even confesses with admirable frankness that it hurt her to be excelled by others. "I have odious little 'inwardnesses' of discomfort when distanced." [51]

Her ambition was as wide as it was intense. Politics?
Oh, yes, certainly politics. "Next to a wish I had to
be a saint some day," she tells an audience, "I really
would like to be a politician."[52] Literature? In youth
she feels an overpowering desire to utter great thoughts
and emotions, which she can never quite put into words.
And all her life the same desire haunted her, so that
the immense realized glory of her public achievement
was never thoroughly satisfying. She would have liked
to write something that the future would have read and
read forever. One curious passage from her "Autobiography" is worth quoting at length, as an illustration
of her mind and temper and also of her frankness of
self-revelation: "Just here I will say, though it is not
usual to reveal one's highest literary ambition, especially when one has failed to attain it, that I am willing
to admit that mine has been during the last thirty years
to write for the 'Atlantic Monthly'! . . . I have written for 'Harper's' and had a letter in the 'Century,'
but I have never yet dared offer one to the 'Atlantic.'
Once I went so far as to send its admired editor,
Thomas Bailey Aldrich, a printed article that I thought
tolerably good, that is for me, asking him if he believed
I could write anything the 'Atlantic' would accept. I
received in reply a courteous note with the enigmatical

statement that he was unable to say from the article forwarded whether I could or not. The question in my mind is now and ever shall be, 'Is that a compliment to the article?' . . . But I give the cultured editor notice that though I may never be lifted to the Olympian heights of his pages, I intend so to live that somebody who is, shall yet write of me between those magic yellow covers of the Queen of Monthlies!"[53]*

Though she wrote vastly, it is hardly to be supposed that Miss Willard's literary reputation is likely to be permanent. It was in the very different field of immediate personal public triumph that she won successes huge enough to satisfy any ambition that could be satisfied at all. It is of the nature of these triumphs that they caress and excite and stimulate the soul more than any others and the study of their effect upon Miss Willard is everywhere extremely curious.

In other words, all through the immense length of her "Autobiography" I think we may perceive, cannot deny, a growing self-consciousness, which I would call vanity, if the word were not misleading. Do not suppose that this is inconsistent with power. Cicero was an enormous power in the world and was one of the vainest of men. It would be folly to speak of Miss

---

* It may be worth noting that with the appearance of this portrait in the *Atlantic* Miss Willard's wish was for the first time gratified.

Willard as vain in comparison with Cicero. Nor is the vanity inconsistent with an almost childlike simplicity. On the contrary, it seems to go with it naturally. It did with Cicero. It did with Miss Willard. Simplicity and a singular charm are not incompatible with vanity at all. Nevertheless, by force of endeavoring to live all one's life as an example one runs a little risk of coming to regard one's life as exemplary, and this danger Miss Willard did not altogether escape. This it is which leads her to expose her soul in page after page with such extraordinary frankness. She meant to do good, no doubt she might do good, and did do good; but one cannot wholly escape the impression of a naturally modest lady undressing in public.

Of course through all the exposure and the stress upon precept there is a constant insistence upon humility. And no one can question for a moment that the humility is genuine. When Miss Willard wrote in her youth: "I think myself not good, not gifted in any way. I cannot see why I should be loved, why I should hope for myself a beautiful and useful life or a glorious immortality at its close,"[54] she meant it. When she wrote in age, "I love too well the good words of the good concerning what I do; I have not the control of tongue and temper that I ought to have, . . . and the sweet south wind of love has not yet thawed out the ice-cake of selfishness from my breast,"[55] she meant it also, even if she might have preferred saying it herself to having any one else say it. Yet even in the humility the subtle and pervading influence of the exemplary life does make itself felt. I know few things more curious than Miss Willard's elaborate study of her own faults for the benefit of the public. After the most thorough and searching investigation, it would appear that she practically finds but two, and of those two one runs eminent risk of finally turning out to be a virtue.[56]

I do not mean, however, to overstress this element of self-consciousness in Miss Willard, which was entirely natural and almost unavoidable in the life she led. But, no matter what may have been the effects of that life upon her character, there can be no question but that she enjoyed it. She herself tells us so. She had magnificent health, cherished by intelligent care and enduring through a long course of years. "Painless, in a world of pain,"[57] she says of herself,—and what a qualification that is for hearty enjoyment! She adds further the notable sentence already quoted: "The chief wonder of my life is that I dare to have so good a time, both physically, mentally and religiously."[58] A good time she certainly did have. All the excitement of the ordinary public entertainer was hers,—the actor, the singer, the performer to huge audiences generally. Everywhere she could count upon an attentive hearing, usually upon an enthusiastic one; and if she had to battle to make it so, the battle, to her temperament, was almost as delightful as the victory. But to the general excitement of the stage and the platform was added the far greater excitement of conscious benevolent motive. You were stirring all these crowds, winning all these plaudits, not for yourself, not for your personal glory, but for a great cause,—for the advancement of good in the world, to hasten the splendid coming of the kingdom of God. Perhaps the psychology of the philanthropist, of the reformer, of the evangelist has yet to be written with minute and analytical care, and he will never be the one to write it himself. But Miss Willard has supplied more curious information on the subject than any one else.

Take the impressive and delightful incident, described by her and by others, of the attack on the Pittsburg saloon by a group of women, all standing in earnest, awed attention along the curbstone, while "a sorrowful old lady, whose only son had gone to ruin through that very deathtrap, knelt on the cold, moist pavement and

offered a broken-hearted prayer." [59]   No doubt these
are the things that move the world, but they also afford
an interest beyond any other for those who take part
in them. Miss Willard, with the best intentions, wished
to deny to everybody the excitement of alcohol. But
she herself lived on the fierce excitement of doing good,
beside which all other stimulants are pale and watery.

IV

I HAVE thus emphasized the vast and varied enjoyment of Miss Willard's life, because so many of her
admirers have called it a life of sacrifice. Of course
she made sacrifices. Who does not? When she chose
her philanthropic career, she gave up a prospect of
assured ease and assured usefulness for a wild and
stormy course which might lead nowhere. And at other
times she gave up other things which were hard to
relinquish. But to call her life a life of sacrifice in
comparison with some other lives would be absurd.
How many women go daily about city streets to relieve
suffering, to comfort misery, to cherish fainting hope,
without any thought of reward or any stimulus of glory,
worn, weary, and discouraged, sacrificing everything to
the sense of duty and the pressure of conscience! How
many women in far country homes live long lives of

utter monotony, drudging over ugly cares, with nothing but grumbling and faultfinding about them, their habit of existence so in-woven with sacrifice that they cannot even imagine the possibility of anything else! Beside these how can any one talk of sacrifice in connection with Frances Elizabeth Willard? If she could have been convinced that she could bring the cause she served to immediate triumph by changing places with one of these women, I think so highly of her that I am sure she would have done it. But what ingenuity she would have shown in resisting the conviction!

Let me repeat, then, that she was a woman of noble character, of splendid and enduring power, one who left the world a legacy of accomplishment which is to-day maturing into the widest and most fruitful results; but she was neither a martyr nor a saint, and, heavens, how she did enjoy herself!

VIII
EMILY DICKINSON

CHRONOLOGY

Emily Dickinson
Born in Amherst, Massachusetts, December 10, 1830.
Lived in Amherst.
Died in Amherst, May 15, 1886.

EMILY DICKINSON

I

ONE who, as a child, knew Emily Dickinson well and loved her much recollects her most vividly as a white, ethereal vision, stepping from her cloistral solitude onto the veranda, daintily unrolling a great length of carpet before her with her foot, strolling down to where the carpet ended among her flowers, then turning back and shutting herself out of the world.

It is just so that we must think of her as coming into the larger world of thought. In the grimmest, austerest background of restrained New England habit and tradition in the mid-nineteenth century there suddenly opens a sunlit door and out steps, floats rather, this white spirit of wonder and grace and fancy and mockery, shakes folly's bells, swings worship's incense, and is gone before we have time to understand her coming.

She, if any one, was in the world, but not of it, not even of the little world which was the only one she lived in. The atmosphere of a New England college town like Amherst is in itself secluded and peculiar with a cloistered charm. Emily's family were secluded in their own souls, even from those who knew them well. Their home was secluded in quiet gravity and dignity. Out of this home, in her years of womanhood, Emily rarely stepped; out of Amherst more rarely still. So perfect was her shy isolation that it seems almost profane to disturb her in it. Yet I have a feeling that she would have wished us to. The shyest, the most isolated, are only waiting, even in their lives, for one to come whose loved approach shall shatter the isolation forever. If the isolation is never shattered, but grows closer and thicker, still I believe that it nurses the hope of a sympathetic, understanding eye that shall see into the most hidden corner of the soul. At any rate, Emily, from her solitude, speaks out to us in puzzling, teasing, witching accents, beckons us, dares us, as it were, to follow her, to seek her, unravel her mystery, lay a searching finger on her heart. Who can resist such a magical solicitation? She speaks to us in strange, chaotic verses, not so much verses as clots of fire, shreds of heaven, snatches of eternity. She speaks to us in letters, chaotic also, but perhaps more fit and helpful for our purpose of approaching her than the poems. We will use the letters to advance with more humdrum steps and now and then get a flash of sudden illumination from the verses.

To begin with, let me re-emphasize the shyness and isolation. She sought it, she loved it. Even in childhood she left home with reluctance and returned with ecstasy. It was not because her inner life was dull and bounded, but because it was vast and wandering; and loved, common things were all that anchored her to herself. "Home," she says, "is the riddle of the wise — the booty of the dove." [1]

She was well aware, of course, of the solitude she lived in. "Nothing has happened but loneliness," she writes to a friend, "perhaps too daily to relate." [2] But you err much if you think the solitude was barren or empty. Light, bright thoughts swarmed in it, quick and eager fancies, wide desires, wider hopes, and endless laughter.

She had books as companions.

> "Unto my books so good to turn
> Far ends of tired days." [3]

To be sure, she was no student, no persistent, systematic reader, as Mrs. Ripley was. She would pick up and put down: a chapter or a page was enough for her, enough to kindle hope or quench ennui, if she ever felt any. But her immense capacity of being stimulated could not resist a book. She loved words, says her niece, Mrs. Bianchi; "the joy of mere words was to Aunt

Emily like red and yellow balls to the juggler."[4] How then could she fail to love the royal masters of words? Her father liked "lonely and rigorous books," she told Colonel Higginson, but she preferred them more graceful or touched with fire. After her first real one, she said to herself, "This, then, is a book, and there are more of them?"[5] When she found Shakespeare, she thought the world needed nothing else.

She had the piano as a companion; played upon it gayly; turned common airs into wild, fantastic reveries, "One improvisation which she called *the Devil* was, by tradition, unparalleled."[6] We may assume that she loved the other arts also, as well as music; at least that they fed her fancy, though her life did not bring her near them.

And nature was the friend of her secluded spirit. "You ask of my companions. Hills, sir, and the sundown, and a dog as large as myself, that my father bought me."[7] Flowers and trees and birds and insects talked to her, and she to them, in that strange speech which they perhaps understood better than her human fellows. What the charm of this converse was she intimates to us in light, delicate touches: "We are having such lovely weather—the air is as sweet and still — now and then a gay leaf falling — the crickets sing all day

long — high in the crimson tree a belated bird is singing." [8]   Or she can go behind this bare portrayal of the
surface and bring out wayward glimpses of hidden feeling, vague and subtle hints of dim emotion such as
flutter in all our spirits and are gone before we can
define them.   She can do this in verse:

> " There 's a certain slant of light,
>   On winter afternoons,
>   That oppresses like the weight
>   Of cathedral tunes." [9]

She can do it even better, to my feeling, in prose: " Nothing is gone, dear, or no one that you knew.   The forests
are at home, the mountains intimate at night and arro-
gant at noon.   A lonesome fluency abroad, like suspended music." [10]

From suggestions such as these it is evident that even
if outside adjuncts failed her wholly, she had sufficient
society in her own thoughts.   She lived in a hurrying
swarm of them, a cloud and tumult of manifold reflections, which made the gross, material contact of daily
human speech and gesture seem poor and common.   She
shut herself off in this silent hurly-burly as in an aristo-
cratic garment of her own.   " How do most people live
without any thoughts?" she cried.   " There are many
people of the world — you must have noticed them in

the street — how they live? How do they get strength
to put on their clothes in the morning?"[11] She herself
put on in the morning a garment of scintillating radiance
and only exchanged it at night for a lighter robe of
gleaming stars. "In a life that stopped guessing you
and I should not feel at home,"[12] she says. She filled
the universe with her guesses and then made comments
on them that were more perplexing than the guesses
were. Not that she was in any way a systematic thinker
any more than reader. Heavens, no! She could never
have labored with the slow and ordered speculations of
Mrs. Ripley. Sometimes she sets up a stable reign of
goodness in the world, believes that things will be well
with us and asserts it hopefully: "I'm afraid we are all
unworthy, yet we shall 'enter in.'"[13] Sometimes she
doubts, rebels even, wonders whether suffering has at
all its due complement of loving; murmurs in wayward
petulence, "It will never look kind to me that God, who
causes all, denies such little wishes."[14] And always, to
her probing guess, the world and life are veiled in mystery, and on the whole she is not ungrateful. "It is true
that the unknown is the largest need of the intellect,
though for it no one thinks to thank God."[15]

It was perhaps, then, dreams that were her playfellows
rather than thoughts, at least thoughts broken, con-

densed, abbreviated, intensified. No doubt she thought
as she spoke and wrote, in gleams and figures, and her
oddities of speech, though they may have been slightly
emphasized by too much Carlyle and Browning; were,
like her oddities of action, not affectations of manner,
but real oddities, quaintnesses, inspired flashes of soul.
She lived in a world of dreams,—dreams above her,
dreams about her, dreams beneath her. Now and then,
as we all do in our rarer moments of half-conscious
somnolence, she rubs her eyes and asks herself of her
condition: "Sometimes I wonder if I ever dreamed—
then if I 'm dreaming now, then if I *always* dreamed." [16]
But the eyes close again, and the dreams press more
thickly, sweet phantoms that crowd and shudder into
one another in the strange, disordered way dreams have.
"The lawn is full of south and the odors tangle, and I
hear to-day for the first [time] the river in the tree." [17]
She tries to clutch them, to stay their dim and fluttering
passage: "I would eat evanescence slowly"; [18] but they
quiver and fade and vanish,only to give place to others
as fantastic and enchanting as themselves.

Yet back of the dream playfellows there is one substance that endures and never fails her,—God, set solid
in the white, unchanging background of eternity. And
I do not say that she had any dry, mental conviction

about these things. When mortal pangs come, they rend and tear her hope as they do others':

> "My life closed twice before its close;
>   It yet remains to see
> If immortality unveil
>   A third event to me,
> So huge, so hopeless to conceive,
>   As these that twice befell.
> Parting is all we know of heaven,
>   And all we need of hell." [19]

And I do not say that God was anything tangible to her, like her father in the next room. If He had been, she would not have found Him God, or loved Him when she had her father. In her quaint, wild way she even indicates that she loved God because He shunned society as she did. "They say that God is everywhere, and yet we always think of Him as somewhat of a recluse." [20] But God filled her solitude, God gave life and body to her dreams, God made evanescence stay with her, or turned evanescence into an all-sustaining, all-enfolding, all-satisfying duration, which made the vague, unquiet futility of common life not only bearable but lovely, even to her restless and inquiring spirit.

Still, for all God and dreams, I would not wholly cut off her image from humanities. "I often wonder how the love of Christ is done when that below holds so." [21] That below held her. Let us see how.

II

IN early life she would seem not to have avoided even general society. There are records of social gatherings, dances, varied merrymakings, in which she took a ready, gay, and active part, without any marked indication of undue withdrawal within herself. In her schooldays she was attractive and, if not exactly popular, could always use her wit and fun to draw listeners and lovers. As a young woman in Amherst, she did not wholly refuse herself to the conventional demands of social inter- course, though it is evident that she yielded with protest and escaped with a sigh of relief: "We go out very little; once in a month or two we both set sail in silks, touch at the principal points and then put into port again. Vinnie cruises about some to transact commerce, but coming to anchor is most I can do." [22] The general kindness of the world, its chilly and indifferent courtesy, its ready and empty acceptance and circulation of cordial nothings grated on her direct and poignant spirit. She would not endure the haggard necessities of parlor conversation. She was suspicious even of real sympathy from an un- authorized source: "Thank you for tenderness. I find that is the only food the Will takes now, — and that, not from general fingers." [23]

But, on the other hand, she had her need of human affection, like every one of us, hungered for it, starved for it at times. She wanted those she loved when she wanted them, wanted them as she wanted them, expected their devotion to her bidding, though she was so coy about doing theirs. When she said come, they were to come, and go, to go. If they did not, it vexed her: "I think I hemmed them faster for knowing you weren't coming, my fingers had nothing else to do.... Odd, that I, who say 'no' so much, cannot bear it from others." [24] She well knew the bounds and limits of friendship; but perhaps she prized it all the more on that account. Her love was as abiding as it was elusive. Grasp it and it flitted away from you. Then it flitted back, like a delicate butterfly, and teased and tantalized your heart with quaint touches of tenderness, till you knew not whether to laugh or weep. "I hold you few I love, till my heart is red as February and purple as March," [25] she murmurs in her strange idiom; and again she flings love wide beyond even the permanence of her own soul, "To live lasts always, but to love is finer than to live." [26]

These things rather for outside friendship. As for her family, she clung to them with the close persistence of a warm burr, which pricks and sticks. She knew all their foibles, of which that stern New England household had enough. She sets them out with the calmest realization, as a keen-sighted heart will, must: "Mother and Margaret are so kind, father as gentle as he knows how, and Vinnie good to me, but 'cannot see why I don't get well'";[27] or in a more general, inimitable picture: "I have a brother and sister; my mother does not care for thought, and father, too busy with his briefs to notice what we do. He buys me many books, but begs me not to read them, because he fears they joggle the mind. They are religious, except me, and address an eclipse, every morning, whom they call their 'Father.'"[28] Yet she loved them all, with a deep, devoted tenderness. Her mother comes to us mainly as a shadow figure, to be petted and spared and cared for. Her sister was a swift, practical personage, not too ready to enjoy Emily's vagaries, but trained to accept them. She swept and dusted and cooked, and tried sometimes to get a useful hand from her dreaming sister, — a useful hand, perhaps, when she got it; but I fancy she often wished she had not. Of the two brothers, Austen was Emily's favorite, or at least she looked up to him as she did to her father, a stern, august, impressive face and spirit. Intimate communion with such a one must have been difficult for anybody. Certainly Emily would not have looked for it nor expected it. But to touch that granite soul and feel that it belonged to you, made life seem more solid and death less terrible.

And the same was far truer of her father. Certainly he never put his cheek or his heart against hers, never fondled her or caressed her. She would not have wished such things, would have resented them. "Father's real life and mine sometimes come into collision," she says, "but as yet escape unhurt."[29] But she looked up to him, how she looked up to him! Or rather, she was always looking up, and in doing so she found her father's face a marked signpost on the way to God.

Yet she could not touch those she loved best, friends, or near, dear kinsfolk. None of us can, you say. To be sure; but she knew it and most of us do not. She moved among her family and through their house like the ghostly shadow of a rare desire. The little needs and calls of domestic duty she detested, though she sometimes took her part in them. Hear her wayward fancy describe that soul's pest, a household removal: "I cannot tell you how we moved. I had rather not remember. I believe my 'effects' were brought in a bandbox, and the 'deathless me,' on foot, not many moments after. I took at the time a memorandum of my several senses, and also of my hat and coat, and my best shoes — but it was lost in the *mêlée,* and I am out with lanterns, looking for myself." [30]   The patient solicitude of nursing tenderness she gave no doubt most deftly and devotedly, yet one feels its burden: "Mother's dear little wants so engross the time . . . I hardly have said 'Good-morning, mother,' when I hear myself saying, 'Mother, good-night.'" [31]

But her isolation from these crying, crowding human realities about her went deeper than the mere irksomeness of daily duty.   The trouble was that they were not realities but shadows, as she herself was, even more. What was sure and reliable and eternal and beyond the touch of trouble, was solitude and loneliness, where she could forever regale herself with the infinite companionship of thought.   These dear human perplexities flitted in unaccountably.   Before you could adjust yourself to them, they were gone, and you were never quite certain whether they left love behind them or torment. "Perhaps death gave me awe for friends, striking sharp and early, for I held them since in a brittle love, of more alarm than peace." [32]

Then one wonders how it was with the greatest love of all, the love of sex for sex.   Did it help her or hurt her or ever come near her?   That she was fitted to draw the love of men is clear enough.   She was strangely, puzzlingly beautiful.   It was not an every-day, peach and cream, ballroom beauty. She teased and startled with her face as with her soul. Her piercing, disconcerting eyes; her rich, gleaming, gold-auburn hair; her white, fragile, ever-stirring, questioning hands; her movements, light and wafted as the movements of a dream, —all these must have tormented men's hearts as the wild suggestion of her words did. We know that she had lovers in the early days, when the world touched her; and the memory of her fairy charm must have haunted many who never thought of spoken love. But how was she herself affected? Did she return the love that came to her, or long to return it, or have a girl's visions of what it might be if it came in all its glory and were returned? The record of these things is dim and vague. In her early youth she looks forward, mockingly, to lovers, and expects to be the belle of Amherst when she reaches her seventeenth year. "Then how I shall delight to make them await my bidding, and with what delight shall I witness their suspense while I make my final decision."[33] Later love calls her to a rapturous hour, though duty forbids and she overcomes the temptation, — "not a glorious victory, where you hear the rolling drum, but a kind of helpless victory, where triumph would come of itself, faintest music, weary soldiers, nor a waving flag, nor a long, loud shout."[34] And through

the letters and through the poems there breathes often
the faint, poignant perfume of love, flickers the wayward, purple flame of love, — love questioning, love ex-
ultant, love despairing, at once immortal and impossible.

But who could realize Emily at the head of a household, a calm, buxom matron, providing her husband's
dinner and ordering the domestic duties? As well yoke
a wood-nymph to the plough. And children — doubtless she loved children, the children of others, played
with them, laughed with them, wept with them. Perhaps children of her own would have been hardly envia-
ble. She was made to dream of all these things, to step
for a moment into the tumult of others' tears and
laughter, always with the protecting carpet daintily unrolled before her feet, then to vanish quietly, visionlike,
back into the blue void, her own inner region, where
there was still that colossal, constant companion, God,
and the echoing silence of eternity.

And if love did not often tempt her out of this solitude, did conscience sometimes urge her out? Did she
feel that the world needed her, that there were deeds to
be done and fights to be won? Did she suffer from that
restless, haunting desire of action which so many of us
misread and call by fine names, but which more or less
overrides almost all of us with its impetuous tyranny?

She perhaps as little as any. But I seem to catch at least some understanding of it in the exquisite, tender solicitation to a doubting heart: "All we are strangers, dear, the world is not acquainted with us, because we are not acquainted with her; and pilgrims. Do you hesitate? And soldiers, oft — some of us victors, but those I do not see to-night, owing to the smoke. We are hungry, and thirsty, sometimes, we are barefoot and cold — will you still come?" [35] But the smoke and the soldiers and the fighting were mostly drowned in quiet — for her.

III

Do not, however, for a moment suppose that because her feet were quiet her mind was, that because she refused to live in the casual world herself she was not interested in the casual life of others. On the contrary, do we not know that these solitary, passionate recluses live all life over in their windowed cells, that it is the wild abundance of other lives in their rioting imaginations that makes all possible adventures of their own seem tame and frigid? Do we not know old Burton, who sucked strange melancholy from the confused chaos that rumbled about him, whose dear delight was to turn from his thumbed folios to the loud, profane quarreling of bargemen by the riverside? Do we not know Flaubert, who shut himself up in his ivory tower, only to lean from his window in the moonlight and hear the dim revelry and causeless laughter of the children of men? So Emily. The action she dreamed of was too vast for the poor, trammeled limits of this world. But she found an absorbed pleasure in watching this world's stumbling, struggling labors, all the same. It was not so much concrete facts, not the contemporary history which seems all-important to those who are making it and mainly dies when they do. Politics? Emily cannot fix her thoughts on politics. "Won't you please tell me when you answer my letter who the candidate for President is? . . . I don't know anything more about affairs in the world than if I were in a trance." [36] But human passion, human love, human hope, and human despair, these absorb her, these distract her, with an inexhaustible interest. She feels them in the touch of human hands and reads them in human faces:

> " I like a look of agony,
>   Because I know it's true;
>   Men do not sham convulsion,
>   Nor simulate a throe." [37]

The thrill of life, its glitter, its color, her eyes and her thoughts were awake for them always: " Friday I tasted life. It was a vast morsel. A circus passed the house

— still I feel the red in my mind though the drums are out." [38]

This vivid sense of the intensity, the ardor, the emotional possibility of things, filled her with passion so overwhelming that it could not be expressed directly. Words were inadequate, and she was obliged to take refuge in jest, mockery, fantastic whim, which merely deepen the message of underlying feeling for those who understand. She was own sister to Charles Lamb in this, — Lamb in whom tears were so close to laughter and the most apparently wanton jesting the cover for a tortured heart. It seems at moments as if Emily mocked everything. She sits idly on the stile in the sunshine and lets the great circus of the world pass by her, riddling its vain parade with shafts of dainty laughter. She is simple, she says, childish, she says, plays all day with trifles, regardless of the mad doings of real men and women. " As simple as you please, the simplest sort of simple — I 'll be a little ninny, a little pussy catty, a little Red Riding Hood; I 'll wear a bee in my bonnet, and a rosebud in my hair, and what remains to do you shall be told hereafter." [39]

She carried the screen of whim not only into verbal mockery, but into strange fancies of capricious action, tricks of Puck and Ariel, which amazed and delighted children and simple hearts, but annoyed and disconcerted the grave, staid, older children who had never grown up to real childishness. She would drop kittens to drown in a pickle jar and shudder with scared glee when they were served up on the hospitable table to a visiting judge.[40] She would say to another grave judge, as Falstaff might have, when the plum-pudding was lighted: "Oh, sir, may one eat of hell fire with impunity here?"[41] And in all these fantastic tricks there was no affectation, though some thought so who did not understand, no affectation in the sense of a conscious effort to impress or astonish. There was no vagary of the witless. It was simply the direct impression of a great, strange world in a heart which could not grasp it and strove to, and gave right back the bewitching oddities it found.

And if this surface of confusing eccentricity might be thought to imply a callous or even cruel indifference to what others took with enormous and bewildered seriousness, it must be repeated and insisted that, as with Lamb, the eccentricity was a mere mask for the most complete and sensitive sympathy, extending often to pity and tears. She was a sister of Lamb. She was also a sister of those most delicate creatures of the whole world's imagination, the clowns of Shakespeare;

and if Touchstone and Feste could not surpass her in exquisite fooling, she was equally akin to the tragic tenderness of the clown in "Lear." It needed all the gayety and all the trifling and all the mad songs to keep down the waves of sorrow that would surge upward in her spirit, and at times not all would do. "If we can get our hearts 'under,' I don't have much to fear — I 've got all but three feelings down, if I can only keep them!" [42]

So, in the effort to explain or forget she mocked at all the grave and busy problems of the world. Love? A divine, unrealizable dream, so tantalizing in its witchery that one could not but make a tender jest of it. Money? Possessions? Oh, the solid, evanescent things! The foundations of our souls rest on them and they slip away and leave us weltering. We *must* make a jest of them too. "You know I should expire of mortification to have our rye-field mortgaged, to say nothing of its falling into the merciless hands of a loco!" [43] And the busy people of the world, the grave, substantial, active, useful people. She is not useful, and she knows it and deplores it. Yet, deploring her own inactivity, she cannot go without her jest at the others: "L—— goes to Sunderland, Wednesday, for a minute or two; leaves here at half-past six — what a fitting hour—and will breakfast the night before; such a smart atmosphere! The trees stand right up straight when they hear her boots, and will bear crockery wares instead of fruit, I fear." [44] And again she sums up this mighty buzz and hum of the achieving world—or the world that dreams it is achieving—with the image of a circus, probably the most vivid form of vain activity that came under her touch: "There is circus here, and farmers' Commencement, and boys and girls from Tripoli, and governors and swords parade the summer streets. They lean upon the fence that guards the quiet church ground, and jar the grass row, warm and soft as a tropic nest." [45] Or a briefer word gives the same vast—to staid souls how hor- rifying!—lesson to a child: "I am glad it is your birthday. It is this little bouquet's birthday too. Its Father is a very old man by the name of Nature, whom you never saw. Be sure to live in vain, dear. I wish I had." [46]

And if she could mock the most serious things of this world, do not suppose that she had the slightest hesita- tion about mocking another. Eternity was so near her always that she treated it as familiarly as her brothers and sisters, and to step out of the wide-open door of death seemed far less of an adventure than to step out

of the grim, closed front door into the streets of Amherst. Ill-health, whether as the prelude to death or
as the torment of life, she could touch lightly. In
strangers she could trifle with it: "Mrs. S. is very
feeble; 'can't bear allopathic treatment, can't have
homœopathic, don't want hydropathic,' oh, what a pickle
she is in!" [47] In her own family she takes it as easily:
"We are sick hardly ever at home, and don't know what
to do when it comes, — wrinkle our little brows, and
stamp with our little feet, and our tiny souls get angry,
and command it to go away." [48] When the blow struck
herself, she may have writhed, but we have nothing to
show it. There is the same mockery to wave it aside:
"My head aches a little, and my heart a little more,
so taking me *collectively*, I seem quite miserable; but
I'll give you the sunny corners, and you mustn't look
at the shade." [49]

Religion, formal religion, Sunday religion, the religion of staid worship and rock-bound creeds, she takes
as airily, with as astonishing whiffs of indifference, not
to say irreverence. If a phrase of scripture, even the
most sacred, fits a jest, she takes it. If a solemn piece
of starched emptiness in the pulpit ruffles her nice and
tender spirit, she does not hesitate to turn him into
delicate and cutting ridicule. Faith, she says, oh, yes,

faith, how august, how venerable! "We dignify our faith when we can cross the ocean with it, though most prefer ships." [50] A revival comes to town. I have no doubt its deeper side stirred her whole soul. But this she cannot put into adequate speech, and instead: "There is that which is called an 'awakening' in the church, and I know of no choicer ecstasy than to see Mrs. —— roll out in crape every morning, I suppose to intimidate antichrist; at least it would have that effect on me." [51]

Even her most intimate friend, her comforter and consoler, her everlasting solace, God, is treated with such light ease as an intimate friend would be. We have seen that every morning her family prayed to an eclipse whom they called their Father. Elsewhere the tone is just the same: "If prayers had any answers to them, you were all here to-night, but I seek and I don't find, and knock and it is not opened. Wonder if God is just—presume He is, however, and 'twas only a blunder of Matthew's." [52] Or, take much the same thing, in apparently more solemn form, but really as daring as Omar Khayyám:

> "'Heavenly Father,' take to thee
> The supreme iniquity,
> Fashioned by thy candid hand
> In a moment contraband.

> Though to trust us seem to us
> More respectful — ' we are dust.'
> We apologize to thee
> For thine own duplicity." [53]

I quote verse here to show that every phase of Emily's thought and character could be illustrated from her poems as well as from her letters. Criticism of the poems as such is not within the limits of my purpose. Yet even the most abstract literary criticism of a writer's works usually serves to give some clue to the writer's mind. And doubtless the puzzling incoherency and complexity of Emily's versicles, the wild vagary of her rhythm and rhyme, express the inner workings of her spirit, as Milton's majestic diction and movement imply the ample grandeur of his soul. Common words come from common lips and rare from rare, and if the rareness verges on oddity in utterance there is oddity in the spirit too. At any rate, it is indisputable that every trait I have been working out in Emily's letters could be found in the poems, also, only more obscure, more veiled, more dubious, more mystical. The love of friends is there and the search for them and the hopeless impossibility of touching them. The longing for love is there, all its mystery, its ravishing revelations and its burden. The intense joy of life is there; its vivid color, its movement, its sparkle, its merriment, its absurdity. There, too, is the turning away from it with vast relief, quiet, solitude, peace, eternity, and God.

It will be asked whether, in writing her vast number of little verses, Emily had any definite idea of literary ambition, of success and glory. Certainly she made no direct effort for anything of the kind. Only three or four poems were printed during her lifetime, and those with extreme reluctance on her part. Her verses were scattered through brief letters, tossed off with apparent indifference and evident disregard of finish. In the main, they must have been rather a form of intense, instinctive expression than a conscious attempt to catch the thoughts and admiration of men. She herself says: "When a sudden light on orchards, or a new fashion in the wind troubled my attention, I felt a palsy here, the verses just relieve." [54] It is true that there are occasional suggestions of literary interest. This is sometimes implied in her intercourse with Colonel Higginson, though I cannot but feel that her correspondence with the good colonel contains more attitude than her other letters, and she certainly played with him a little. Further, the verses which introduce the first volume of poems are definitely in the nature of an author's apology:

> "This is my letter to the world,
> That never wrote to me."

Nevertheless, we are safe in saying that few authors have left permanent work with so little conscious preoccupation of authorship.

IV

AND so we are brought back to her one great preoccupation with the inner life and God and eternity; for eternity rings through every thought of her, like a deep and solemn bell, monotonous, if its surface echoes were not broken into such wild and varied music. Change? She appreciates change, no one more keenly, its glory and its horror. "No part of mind is permanent. This startles the happy, but it assists the sad."[55] Rest? She appreciates rest, if in this world there were such a thing. Love "makes but one mistake, it tells us it is 'rest'—perhaps its toil is rest, but what we have not known we shall know again, that divine 'again' for which we are all breathless."[56] But change and toil and love and agony, all she forgets in that divine permanence, from which her soul cannot escape and does not desire to.

> "As all the heavens were a bell,
> And Being but an ear,
> And I and silence some strange race,
> Wrecked, solitary, here."[57]

Or, again, in prose, even more simple and overwhelming: "I cannot tell how Eternity seems. It sweeps around me like a sea." [58]

Let no one say that this inner absorption, this dwelling with God and with that which abideth, is selfish. Many will say so. And what lives do they lead themselves? Lives of empty bustle, of greedy haste, of futile activity and eagerness. Lives, no doubt, also of wide usefulness and deep human sacrifice; but these are not the most ready to accuse others. And too often broad social contact and a constant movement out of doors are but symptoms of emptiness, of hatred of solitude, of an underlying fear of one's self and of being left alone with God.

Who shall say that such a quiet, self-contained, self-filling life as Emily Dickinson's, with its contagion of eternity spreading ineffably from soul to soul, is not in the end as useful for example and accomplishment as the buzz existence of Mrs. Stowe or Frances Willard?

It is true that some who watched her thought her selfish in minor matters. She was exacting with her family, made hard demands and expected to have them satisfied. But this was a detail. In her larger life she forgot self altogether, or rather, she made self as wide as heaven, till all loves and all hates and all men and all God were included in it.   And note that she did not fly the world for her own purposes.   She had no aim of long ambition to work out in solitude.   She did not trouble with self-culture, did not buttress thought upon the vast security of books and learning, as did Mrs. Ripley.   She just sat quiet, with the doors of her spirit open, and let God come to her.   And even that celestial coming did not make her restless.   She had not Mary Lyon's longing to bring God to others.   She did not share Frances Willard's passionate cry, "tell every one to be good."   If God had desired men to be good, He would have made them so.   If God's world needed mending, let Him mend it.   She knew well enough He could, if He wished.   Why should she vex her soul with trifles?   For to her was not the real unreal and the unreal real?

So I see her last as I saw her first, standing, all white, at her balcony window, ready to float downward upon her unrolled carpet into the wide garden of the world, holding eternity clutched tight in one hand and from the other dropping with idle grace those flower joys of life which the grosser herd of us run after so madly.   And I hear her brothers, the clowns of Shakespeare, singing:

"When that I was and a little, tiny boy,
　With heigh-ho, the wind and the rain,
A little thing was all my joy.
　For the rain it raineth every day.

"When that I had and a little, tiny wit,
　With heigh-ho, the wind and the rain,
I made content with my fortunes fit.
　For the rain it raineth every day." [59]

THE END

NOTES

TITLES OF BOOKS MOST FREQUENTLY CITED
SHOWING ABBREVIATIONS USED

Adams, Abigail — *Letters,* 2 vols. — *Letters.*

Adams, Abigail — *Familiar Letters.* — *Familiar Letters.*

Bianchi, Martha Dickinson — Selections from the unpublished letters of Emily Dickinson to her brother's family, in the *Atlantic Monthly,* vol. cxv, p. 35. — Mrs. Bianchi.

Cheney, Ednah Dow — *Reminiscences.* — Mrs. Cheney—*Rem.*

Cheney, Ednah Dow — *Louisa May Alcott, Her Life, Letters, and Journals,* edited by Ednah D. Cheney. — Mrs. Cheney.

Dickinson, Emily — *Letters of Emily Dickinson,* edited by Mabel Loomis Todd, in 2 vols. — *Letters.*

Dickinson, Emily — *Poems, First, Second* and *Third Series.* — *Poems,* I, II, III.

Dickinson, Emily — *The Single Hound.* — *The Single Hound.*

Fields, Annie — *Life and Letters of Harriet Beecher Stowe.* — Mrs. Fields.

Fisk, Fidelia — *Recollections of Mary Lyon, with Selections from her Instructions to the Pupils in Mount Holyoke Female Seminary.* — Miss Fisk.

Fuller, Sarah Margaret — *Love Letters.* — *Love Letters.*

Fuller, Sarah Margaret — *Memoirs,* 2 vols. — *Memoirs.*

Gilchrist, Beth Bradford — *Life of Mary Lyon.* — Miss Gilchrist.

Gordon, Anna A. — *The Beautiful Life of Frances E. Willard.* — *Life.*

Higginson, Thomas Wentworth — *Margaret Fuller Ossoli.* — Higginson.

Hitchcock, Edward — *The Power of Christian Benevolence illustrated in the Life and Labors of Mary Lyon.* — Hitchcock.

Manuscript in Boston Public Library. — MS., B. P. L.

Reminiscences of Mary Lyon by her Pupils — Manuscript in Mount Holyoke Library. — *Reminiscences.*

Stowe, Charles E. — *The Life of Harriet Beecher Stowe.*   Stowe.

Stowe, Charles E. and Lyman B. — *Harriet Beecher Stowe.*   Stowe and Stowe.

Willard, Frances E. — *Gimpses of Fifty Years.*   Glimpses.

NOTES

CHAPTER I: ABIGAIL ADAMS

1. *Letters*, vol. II, p. 29.
2. *Familiar Letters*, p. 182.
3. *Familiar Letters*, p. 126.
4. *Letters*, vol. I, p. 187.
5. *Letters*, vol. II, p. 269.
6. *Letters*, vol. II, p. 265.
7. *Letters*, vol. I, p. 185.
8. *Familiar Letters*, p. 26.
9. *Letters*, vol. II, p. 219.
10. *Familiar Letters*, p. 159.
11. *Familiar Letters*, p. 355.
12. John Quincy Adams, *Memoirs*, vol. IV, p. 155.
13. John Quincy Adams, *Memoirs*, vol. IV, p. 157.
14. John Quincy Adams, *Memoirs*, vol. XI, p. 400.
15. Abigail Adams (Smith), *Journal and Correspondence*, p. 215.
16. *Letters*, vol. II, p. 56.
17. *Letters*, vol. II, p. 186.
18. *Familiar Letters*, p. 64.
19. *Familiar Letters*, p. 351.
20. *Familiar Letters*, p. 253.
21. *Familiar Letters*, p. 368.
22. *Familiar Letters*, p. 125.
23. *Familiar Letters*, p. 179.
24. *Familiar Letters*, preface, p. xxvii.
25. *Familiar Letters*, p. 244.
26. *Warren-Adams Letters*, vol. I, p. 19.
27. *Familiar Letters*, p. 122.
28. *Familiar Letters*, p. 150.
29. *Letters*, vol. II, p. 229.
30. *Letters*, vol. II, p. 271.
31. Abigail Adams (Smith), *Journal and Correspondence*, p. 216.
32. *Letters*, vol. II, p. 16.
33. *Letters*, vol. II, p. 5.
34. *Familiar Letters*, p. 310.
35. *Familiar Letters*, p. 10.
36. *Familiar Letters*, p. 130.
37. *Familiar Letters*, p. 361.
38. *Letters*, vol. II, p. 264.
39. *Familiar Letters*, p. 53.
40. *Familiar Letters*, p. 69.
41. *Familiar Letters*, p. 52.
42. *Familiar Letters*, p. 384.
43. *Familiar Letters*, p. 309.
44. *Familiar Letters*, p. 138.
45. Abigail Adams (Smith), *Journal and Correspondence*, p. 223.
46. *Familiar Letters*, p. 42.
47. *Familiar Letters*, p. 91.
48. *Familiar Letters*, p. 229.
49. *Familiar Letters*, p. 47.
50. *Familiar Letters*, p. 214.
51. John Adams, *Works*, vol. X, p. 220.
52. *Familiar Letters*, p. 397.
53. John Adams, *Works*, vol. III, p. 418.
54. *Familiar Letters*, p. 121.
55. Abigail Adams (Smith), *Journal and Correspondence*, p. 246.
56. *Letters*, vol. II, p. 235.
57. Abigail Adams (Smith), *Journal and Correspondence*, p. 237.
58. *Works* (Ford), vol. V, p. 14.
59. *Letters*, vol. II, p. 253.
60. *Familiar Letters*, p. 115.

61. *Familiar Letters,* p. 367.
62. *Familiar Letters,* p. 358.
63. *Familiar Letters,* p. 343.

64. *Familiar Letters,* p. 201.
65. *Familiar Letters,* p. 79.
66. *Familiar Letters,* p. 411.

CHAPTER II: SARAH ALDEN RIPLEY

With trifling exceptions, the quotations used in the portrait of Mrs. Ripley are taken either from manuscript sources or from the comparatively brief sketch of her by Miss Elizabeth Hoar, printed in *Worthy Women of Our First Century,* Philadelphia, 1888.

CHAPTER III: MARY LYON

1. Miss Gilchrist, p. 32.
2. Miss Gilchrist, p. 29.
3. Miss Gilchrist, p. 59.
4. Miss Gilchrist, p. 313.
5. Miss Gilchrist, p. 54.
6. Miss Gilchrist, p. 123.
7. Miss Gilchrist, p. 82.
8. Miss Gilchrist, p. 120.
9. Hitchcock, p. 172.
10. Miss Gilchrist, p. 203.
11. Miss Gilchrist, p. 217.
12. Miss Gilchrist, p. 227.
13. Miss Gilchrist, p. 232.
14. Miss Gilchrist, p. 247.
15. Hitchcock, p. 246.
16. Miss Gilchrist, p. 232.
17. Miss Gilchrist, p. 240.
18. Miss Gilchrist, p. 234.
19. Miss Gilchrist, p. 235.
20. Miss Gilchrist, p. 232.
21. Miss Gilchrist, p. 241.
22. Miss Gilchrist, p. 342.
23. Hitchcock, p. 87.
24. Miss Gilchrist, p. 248.
25. Miss Gilchrist, p. 314.
26. Miss Gilchrist, p. 316.
27. *Reminiscences,* p. 42.
28. Hitchcock, p. 144.
29. Miss Gilchrist, p. 391.
30. Miss Gilchrist, p. 150.
31. Miss Fisk, p. 153.
32. Miss Gilchrist, p. 316.
33. Hitchcock, p. 75.
34. Miss Gilchrist, p. 133.
35. *Reminiscences,* p. 80.
36. Miss Gilchrist, p. 150.
37. MS., letter, Mt. Holyoke College Library.
38. *Reminiscences,* p. 157.
39. Miss Gilchrist, p. 375.
40. Miss Gilchrist, p. 134.
41. Miss Fisk, p. 327.
42. *Reminiscences,* p. 166.
43. *Reminiscences,* p. 42.
44. Miss Fisk, p. 328.
45. *Ibid.*
46. Hitchcock, p. 284.
47. Miss Gilchrist, p. 86.
48. Miss Gilchrist, p. 127.
49. Miss Gilchrist, p. 389.
50. Miss Gilchrist, p. 115.
51. Miss Gilchrist, p. 116.
52. Miss Gilchrist, p. 82.
53. Miss Fisk, p. 331.
54. Miss Gilchrist, p. 90.
55. Miss Gilchrist, p. 292.

56. Hitchcock, p. 77.
57. *Reminiscences,* p. 168.
58. Miss Gilchrist, p. 198.
59. Hitchcock, p. 103.
60. Hitchcock, p. 81.
61. Hitchcock, p. 44.
62. Hitchcock, p. 80.
63. Hitchcock, p. 389.
64. Hitchcock, p. 331.
65. *Reminiscences,* p. 40.

66. Miss Fisk, p. 236.
67. Miss Fisk, p. 319.
68. Hitchcock, p. 154.
69. Hitchcock, p. 155.
70. Miss Fisk, p. 325.
71. Miss Gilchrist, p. 320.
72. Hitchcock, p. 120.
73. Hitchcock, p. 83.
74. Miss Gilchrist, p. 129.

CHAPTER IV: HARRIET BEECHER STOWE

References for pages of Mrs. Stowe's own works are to Riverside edition, unless otherwise specified.

1. Mrs. Fields, p. 92.
2. Mrs. Fields, p. 69.
3. Stowe and Stowe, p. 77.
4. Mrs. Fields, p. 113.
5. Mrs. Fields, p. 124.
6. Mrs. Fields, p. 115.
7. Mrs. Fields, p. 248.
8. Mrs. Fields, p. 114.
9. Mrs. Fields, p. 70.
10. Mrs. Fields, p. 74.
11. Mrs. Fields, p. 364.
12. Mrs. Fields, p. 72.
13. *Minister's Wooing,* p. 284.
14. Mrs. Fields, p. 97.
15. Stowe, p. 40.
16. Mrs. Fields, p. 91.
17. *Oldtown Folks,* vol. I, p. 29.
18. *Oldtown Folks,* vol. II, p. 54.
19. Stowe and Stowe, p. 59.
20. Mrs. Fields, p. 81.
21. Mrs. Fields, p. 51.
22. Mrs. Fields, p. 68.
23. Mrs. Fields, p. 82.
24. Mrs. Fields, p. 29.
25. Stowe, p. 58.
26. *Footsteps of the Master,* p. 80.

27. Mrs. Fields, p. 290.
28. Stowe, p. 400.
29. E. S. Phelps, in *McClure's Magazine,* vol. VII, p. 7.
30. Mrs. Fields, p. 90.
31. Mrs. Fields, p. 311.
32. Mrs. Fields, p. 146.
33. Mrs. Fields, p. 327.
34. Mrs. Fields, p. 26.
35. Mrs. Fields, p. 49.
36. Stowe and Stowe, p. 59.
37. Mrs. Fields, p. 30.
38. Stowe and Stowe, p. 166.
39. Stowe and Stowe, p. 179.
40. Mrs. Fields, p. 250.
41. Mrs. Fields, p. 185.
42. Stowe and Stowe, p. 256.
43. *Sunny Memories,* vol. II, p. 47, edition 1854.
44. Mrs. Fields, p. 40.
45. Stowe and Stowe, p. 7.
46. Mrs. Fields, p. 341.
47. *Sunny Memories,* vol. II, p. 392, edition 1854.
48. *Sunny Memories,* vol. I, p. 281, edition 1854.

CHAPTER V: MARGARET FULLER OSSOLI

1. Mrs. Cheney, *Rem.,* p. 193.
2. *Memoirs,* vol. I, p. 202.
3. *Memoirs,* vol. I, p. 229.
4. Higginson, p. 11.
5. *Memoirs,* vol. I, p. 65.
6. James Russell Lowell, *Letters,* vol. I, p. 128.
7. Higginson, p. 209.
8. *Love Letters,* p. 20.
9. *Memoirs,* vol. I, p. 234.
10. Higginson, p. 117.
11. Higginson, p. 303.
12. *Memoirs,* vol. I, p. 237.
13. Horace Greeley, *Recollections of a Busy Life,* p. 179.
14. *Memoirs,* vol. I, p. 43.
15. *Memoirs,* vol. I, p. 203.
16. *Memoirs,* vol. I, p. 200.
17. Horace Greeley, *Recollections of a Busy Life,* p. 181.
18. Ralph Waldo Emerson, *Journals,* vol. VI, p. 366.
19. *Ibid.*
20. *Memoirs,* vol. I, p. 298.
21. Higginson, p. 306.
22. *Memoirs,* vol. I, p. 236.
23. Mrs. Cheney, *Rem.,* p. 205.
24. *Memoirs,* vol. I, p. 214.
25. Horace Greeley, *Recollections of a Busy Life,* p. 179.
26. *Love Letters,* p. 30.
27. Mrs. Cheney, *Rem.,* p. 207.
28. *Memoirs,* vol. I, p. 206.
29. *Memoirs,* vol. I, p. 303.
30. Higginson, p. 66.
31. Higginson, p. 289.
32. *Love Letters,* p. 28.
33. Higginson, p. 100.
34. Higginson, p. 59.
35. *Memoirs,* vol. II, p. 97.
36. *Love Letters,* p. 128.
37. *Memoirs,* vol. II, p. 111.
38. Julian Hawthorne, *Nathaniel Hawthorne and His Wife,* vol. I, p. 261.
39. Mrs. Cheney, *Rem.,* p. 210. Mrs. Cheney quotes the words without saying explicitly that they are Margaret's. A fine phrase in any case.
40. *Memoirs,* vol. I, p. 132.
41. Hedge MS.
42. Higginson, p. 64.
43. Higginson, p. 99.
44. Higginson, p. 123.
45. Hedge MS.
46. Hedge MS.
47. Frederick Augustus Braun, *Margaret Fuller and Goethe,* p. 255.
48. *Memoirs,* vol. II, p. 60.
49. *Love Letters,* p. 131.
50. *Memoirs,* vol. II, p. 173.
51. Higginson, p. 307.
52. *Memoirs,* vol. II, p. 53.
53. Higginson, p. 28.
54. Higginson, p. 55.
55. *Memoirs,* vol. II, p. 288.
56. MS., B. P. L. The complete distortion of this passage in *Memoirs,* vol. II, p. 301, is an interesting instance of the unreliability of printed texts.
57. Higginson, p. 104.
58. Higginson, p. 31.
59. *Memoirs,* vol. I, p. 281.
60. *Memoirs,* vol. II, p. 67.
61. *Memoirs,* vol. I, p. 288.
62. *Ibid.*
63. *Love Letters,* p. 100.
64. *Love Letters,* p. 130.
65. *Love Letters,* p. 187.

66. Julian Hawthorne, *Nathaniel Hawthorne and His Wife,* vol. I, p. 259.
67. F. B. Sanborn, *Recollections of Seventy Years,* vol. II, p. 412.
68. MS., B. P. L.
69. *Memoirs,* vol. II, p. 294.
70. MS., B. P. L.
71. *Memoirs,* vol. II, p. 264.
72. *Memoirs,* vol. II, p. 286.
73. MS., B. P. L.
74. MS., B. P. L.
75. MS., B. P. L.

CHAPTER VI: LOUISA MAY ALCOTT

1. Mrs. Cheney, p. 49.
2. Mrs. Cheney, p. 39.
3. Mrs. Cheney, p. 108.
4. Mrs. Cheney, p. 169.
5. Mrs. Cheney, p. 63.
6. Mrs. Cheney, p. 198.
7. *Little Women,* chapter XXXIV.
8. *Little Women,* chapter XXX.
9. Mrs. Cheney, p. 389.
10. Mrs. Cheney, p. 321.
11. Mrs. Cheney, p. 159.
12. Mrs. Cheney, p. 201.
13. *Little Women,* chapter XXIX.
14. Mrs. Cheney, p. 199.
15. Mrs. Cheney, p. 169.
16. Mrs. Cheney, p. 316.
17. To Maria S. Porter, in *New England Magazine,* New Series, vol. VI, p. 4.
18. From Mrs. Alcott's Journal, in *Life of A. Bronson Alcott,* by F. B. Sanborn and William T. Harris, vol. II, p. 473.
19. Mrs. Cheney, p. 300.
20. Mrs. Cheney, p. 198.
21. *Little Women,* chapter XLVII.
22. Mrs. Cheney, p. 116.
23. Mrs. Cheney, p. 37.
24. Mrs. Cheney, p. 89.
25. *Recollections of My Childhood,* in Lulu's Library, vol. III.
26. Mrs. Cheney, p. 357.
27. *Shawl Straps,* chapter V.
28. *Ibid.*
29. Mrs. Cheney, p. 45.
30. Mrs. Cheney, p. 88.
31. *Ibid.*
32. Mrs. Cheney, p. 179.
33. *Poppy's Pranks.*
34. *Recollections of my Childhood,* in Lulu's Library, vol. III.
35. Mrs. Cheney, p. 109.
36. Mrs. Cheney, p. 81.
37. *Hospital Sketches,* postscript.
38. Mrs. Cheney, p. 156.
39. Mrs. Cheney, p. 60.
40. Mrs. Cheney, p. 101.
41. *Work,* chapter VII.
42. Mrs. Cheney, p. 94.
43. *Ibid.*
44. Mrs. Cheney, p. 166.
45. Mrs. Cheney, p. 197.
46. Mrs. Cheney, p. 60.
47. Mrs. Cheney, p. 95.
48. Mrs. Cheney, p. 88.
49. Mrs. Cheney, p. 326.
50. Mrs. Cheney, p. 352.
51. Mrs. Cheney, p. 399.
52. Mrs. Cheney, p. 125.
53. Mrs. Cheney, p. 159.
54. Mrs. Cheney, p. 270.
55. Mrs. Cheney, p. 127.
56. Mrs. Cheney, p. 169.
57. Mrs. Cheney, p. 152.
58. Mrs. Cheney, p. 270.
59. Mrs. Cheney, p. 45.
60. Mrs. Cheney, p. 273.
61. Mrs. Cheney, p. 83.

62. Mrs. Cheney, p. 108.
63. Mrs. Cheney, p. 131.
64. Mrs. Cheney, p. 89.
65. Mrs. Cheney, p. 370.
66. Mrs. Cheney, p. 209.
67. Mrs. Cheney, p. 202.
68. Mrs. Cheney, p. 105.

69. Mrs. Cheney, p. 272.
70. Mrs. Cheney, p. 227.
71. *Hospital Sketches*, chapter III.
72. *Hospital Sketches*, chapter IV.
73. Mrs. Cheney, p. 262.
74. *Correspondance de Voltaire, édition* 1881, vol. XI, p. 168.

CHAPTER VII: FRANCES ELIZABETH WILLARD

1. *Glimpses*, p. 660.
2. *Glimpses*, p. 4.
3. *Glimpses*, pp. 125, 144.
4. *Glimpses*, p. 633.
5. *Glimpses*, p. 4.
6. *Glimpses*, p. 133.
7. *Glimpses*, p. 77.
8. *Glimpses*, p. 109.
9. *Glimpses*, p. 333.
10. *Glimpses*, p. 687.
11. To Mrs. Sarah Knowles Bolton, MS.
12. *Glimpses*, p. 151.
13. *Glimpses*, p. 153.
14. *Glimpses*, p. 125.
15. *Life*, p. 40.
16. *Glimpses*, p. 149.
17. *Glimpses*, p. 645.
18. *Glimpses*, p. 72.
19. *Glimpses*, p. 127.
20. *Glimpses*, p. 159.
21. *Glimpses*, p. 103.
22. *Glimpses*, p. 168.
23. *Glimpses*, p. 170.
24. *Glimpses*, p. 177.
25. *Glimpses*, p. 113.
26. Mary R. Parkman, *Heroines of Service*, p. 111.
27. *Glimpses*, p. 129.
28. *Glimpses*, p. 363.
29. *Glimpses*, p. 686.
30. *Glimpses*, p. 633.
31. *A Life of Service, Sketches of Frances E. Willard*, p. 18.

32. *Glimpses*, p. 689.
33. *A Life of Service, Sketches of Frances E. Willard*, p. 28.
34. *Life*, p. 318.
35. *A Life of Service, Sketches of Frances E. Willard*, p. 15.
36. *Glimpses*, p. 68.
37. *Glimpses*, p. 131.
38. *Glimpses*, p. 518.
39. *Life*, p. 55.
40. *A Life of Service, Sketches of Frances E. Willard*, p. 15.
41. Hannah Whitall Smith, in *Glimpses, Introduction*, p. v.
42. *Life*, p. 318.
43. *Glimpses, Introduction*, p. vi.
44. *Life*, p. 398.
45. *Glimpses*, p. 9.
46. *Glimpses*, p. 230.
47. *Glimpses*, p. 492.
48. *Glimpses, Introduction*, p. v.
49. *Glimpses*, p. 687.
50. *Glimpses*, p. 625.
51. *Glimpses*, p. 690.
52. *Glimpses*, p. 593.
53. *Glimpses*, p. 499.
54. *Glimpses*, p. 125.
55. *Glimpses*, p. 627.
56. *Glimpses*, pp. 646-649.
57. *Glimpses*, p. 632.
58. *Glimpses*, p. 633.
59. *Glimpses*, p. 340.

CHAPTER VIII: EMILY DICKINSON

1. *Letters*, p. 294.
2. *Letters*, p. 248.
3. *Poems*, II, p. 74.
4. Mrs. Bianchi, p. 40.
5. T. W. Higginson, in the *Atlantic Monthly*, vol. LXVIII, p. 452.
6. *Poems, The Single Hound*, p. xi.
7. *Letters*, p. 302.
8. *Letters*, p. 94.
9. *Poems*, I, p. 106.
10. Mrs. Bianchi, p. 41.
11. T. W. Higginson, in the *Atlantic Monthly*, vol. LXVIII, p. 453.
12. Mrs. Bianchi, p. 42.
13. *Letters*, p. 52.
14. *Letters*, p. 237.
15. *Letters*, p. 282.
16. *Letters*, p. 164.
17. *Letters*, p. 171.
18. *Ibid.*
19. *Poems*, III, p. 26.
20. *Letters*, p. 181.
21. *Letters*, p. 205.
22. Mrs. Bianchi, p. 40.
23. Mrs. Bianchi, p. 37.
24. *Letters*, p. 240.
25. *Letters*, p. 169.
26. Mrs. Bianchi, p. 37.
27. *Letters*, p. 255.
28. *Letters*, p. 302.
29. *Letters*, p. 104.
30. *Letters*, p. 167.
31. *Letters*, p. 294.
32. *Letters*, p. 309.
33. *Letters*, p. 6.
34. *Letters*, p. 48.
35. *Letters*, p. 147.
36. *Letters*, p. 67.
37. *Poems*, I, p. 121.
38. *Letters*, p. 171.
39. *Letters*, p. 86.
40. *The Single Hound*, preface, p. xii.
41. *The Single Hound*, preface, p. xiv.
42. *Letters*, p. 76.
43. *Letters*, p. 67.
44. *Letters*, p. 249.
45. MS., letter in possession of Mr. Macgregor Jenkins.
46. Mrs. Bianchi, p. 37.
47. *Letters*, p. 106.
48. *Letters*, p. 47.
49. *Letters*, p. 62.
50. *Letters*, p. 149.
51. *Letters*, p. 279.
52. *Letters*, p. 157.
53. *The Single Hound*, p. 108.
54. *Letters*, p. 303.
55. *Letters*, p. 265.
56. *Letters*, p. 223.
57. *Poems*, III, p. 168.
58. *Letters*, p. 295.
59. Second Stanza of the Shakespeare Lyric has been slightly altered to conform with the first.

INDEX

INDEX

New England conscience, the, 124.

Ossoli, Margaret Fuller, 133; her personal appearance, 134; her four-square egotism, 135–37, 145, 146; could be all things to all men, 137, 138; her power of stimulation, 139–41; her faculty of eliciting confession, 142; her gift of analysis, 144, 145; her studies, 148–50; her *Credo*, 151; her appreciation of nature, 152, 153; her place in literature, 153, 154; always a lover, 154–61; a prudent manager, 155; her relation with Emerson, 156, 157; marriage to Marquis Ossoli, 159; birth of her son, 160; in the Italian revolution, 161, 162; lost in shipwreck, 163.

Ossoli, Marquis, husband of Margaret Fuller, 159.

Pater, Walter, *Imaginary Portrait*, Sebastian van Stork quoted, 64.
Penn's Hill, 19.
Phelps, Elizabeth Stuart, anecdote of Mrs. Stowe, 117.

Religion: Abigail Adams abhorred bigotry, 15; Mrs. Ripley's religious experiences, 38, 51, 52, 58, 59, 61, 62; Mary Lyon's attitude toward, 92–97; the great activity of Mrs. Stowe, 109–14; literature the natural expression for preaching, 117; Margaret Fuller's *Credo*, 151; Louisa Alcott a preacher, 187, 188; Frances Willard's religion an art, 207; Emily Dickinson's attitude toward religion, 235, 236, 250, 251, 255, 256.

Ripley, Sarah Alden, her passion for all kinds of study, 35, 36, 47, 88; her freedom from conventional habit, 37, 38; her religious independence, 38; her freedom from pedantry, 39, 40; early death of her mother, 40; her consequent house-hold cares, 40; her analysis of people, 41, 42; her marriage to Samuel Ripley, 43; prominence of sorrow in her old age, 45; her affection for her home circle, 47, 48; quoted, 49; relinquished a life of study for one of housekeeping, 50; her life as a clergyman's wife, 51, 52; teaching, 53–55; her pupils' love for her, 55; her thirst for pure knowledge, 57, 58; her skepticism, 58, 59; her skepticism contrasted with Emerson's faith, 61, 62; her love of study entirely disinterested, 63, 64.

Rollin's *Ancient History*, 7.
Rubens, Peter Paul, Mrs. Stowe's conversion to, 128.
Russell, Lady, Abigail Adams comparable to, 24.

Sainte-Beuve, quoted, 47.
Sévigné, Madame de, Abigail Adams comparable to, 6, 10.
Shakespeare's clowns, brothers to Emily Dickinson, 247, 248, 256.
Staal-Delaunay, Madame de, Mrs. Stowe's contrast to, 105.
Stowe, Prof. Calvin E., husband of Harriet Beecher, 108.
Stowe, Harriet Beecher, born and grew up in religious atmosphere, 101; her nervous temperament, 102–04; her liking for people reciprocated, 105, 121; her passionate yet reserved nature, 107; not a great scholar, 108, 109; religion her great concern, 109–14; her desire to "do something," 114–16; the pen her best implement, 117–20; her success, 121, 122; a student of character and manners, 123, 124; a furious preacher, 125–27; her part in the Byron controversy, 126; a sunny, human person, 127; her sense of beauty, 128, 129.

Thoreau, H. D., 58.
Trollope, Anthony, quoted, 125.